Eclectic Writings

Man's Strategy for Faith and Elevated
Thoughts of Life

A. Richard McGinnis

BOOKS
ACADEMY
LEARNING LIFE FROM EVERY PAGE

Books Academy LLC
112 SW H K Dodgen Loop,
Temple, Texas 76504
Hotline: (254) 800-1189

Ordering Information:
Quantity sales. Special discounts are available on quantity purchases by corporations, associations, and others. For details, contact the publisher at the address above.

Printed in the United States of America.

ISBN-13: Softcover   978-1-964929-47-7
          eBook   978-1-964929-48-4

Library of Congress Control Number:

Table of Contents

Dedication

I dedicate this manuscript to those in my life who continue to instill love, loyalty, and devotion in me. I include my loving wife, Diana, and my two beautiful daughters, Carrie and Tara who continue to support me throughout this endeavor. I wish to acknowledge my loving brother and sister, Eugene McGinnis, and Ruth Ann McGinnis Stallworth, who provided material for some of my short stories.

First and foremost, I dedicate my life to God, who provided me with endless love and everlasting life when I believed in His Son, the Lord Jesus Christ who died on a cross to save me when I confessed my sins to Him.

POETRY FOR THE PROLETARIAT

The Purpose of Dreams

When you are mellow and sleep leads to
an exhausted feeling in your soul;
You might wonder why you dream of butterflies,
puppies, or a girl on a pole.
Some dreams are nightmares with uncanny
characters chasing you into a pit,
But God has a purpose, and you dream dreams
in a more trustworthy spirit.

My wife dreamed of snakes biting her arm and
the smell of venom was real;
She woke up calling for help with a lacerated
bleeding arm she could not feel.
I awoke and consoled her to decisively make
her understand she would heal.
God's purpose for the dream was to urge me to
hug her and that is His will.

I dreamed of an attack by a Native American
who thrust a spear into my chest;
It was a memorable dream years ago as a child,
but I can't remember the rest.
The thud of the spear pierced deep into my
chest, and I can't forget the mess;
God told me to avoid heart disease, be active,
and focus on healthiness.

I dreamed of crossing a brook in a facile manner
while hiking at Spruce Knob;
There were no problems till I fell in the water,
broke my leg, and lost my job.
I worked as a tour guide walking through
buildings and the loss made me sob;
But the next week I found promising
employment, and I knew it was from God.

My door of opportunity will open soon to
expose prodigious fortune for me;
It is connected in some way with my dream of
sitting on my father's knee.
My life is replete, but the interpretation of
dreams and nightmares is the key;
God helped me understand that the love of my
family is wealth for me.

Age of the Author

The years have passed, and age is making
wrinkles appear;
These lines in my face are telling me that my
end may be near.

What good can I do here to make this world a
better place for others?
I will write poetry for reading and inspire them
like their mother.

The words are locked in my mind, and I will
squeeze them out;
Ideas appear as challenging thoughts as I say
these words aloud.

I write to express my thoughts while traveling
during special trips;
The experiences are important to me, and I
record them as I sit.

The words I write may reveal my age as the tone
of the poetry is serious;
So, I'll change my intent and add gaiety to
make you think I'm delirious.

The reader of prose can be wrapped in the
various characters portrayed;
But these words from an older author will give
you a much better day.

Depression is the Shell of a Nut

I am depressed nearly all day, so I sleep much
of the time;
My loving husband always listens to me when
we dine.
Help me to understand why I am bi-polar and
why others are not;
Depression takes the wind from my sails and
ties them into a knot.

My home is atrocious with litter through the
halls and in each room
Your first response is "Lady, go to the store
and buy a broom!"
No one knows how terrible I feel when I wake
up late in the day;
I would not wish this horrible disease on anyone
to make them pay.
They call it bi-polar, and you know it as maniac
depressive disorder;

When the feelings come to life they are as real
as bricks and mortar.
I have hit a brick wall more times than I want
to count,
I work with my boss to keep him off my back
without a single sound.

I have no friends I can call for assistance when
the going gets rough;
I would rather watch old movies and read while
I sit on my duff.
The depressive part of bi-polar is slowly taking
me away from here;
I cannot find the words to explain this to my
family or my peers.

Before seeing a professional about my condition,
I knew I was a nut,
I knew that compared to the life of others; my
life was in a boring rut.
Now help has arrived and I am happy I have a
therapist I can call;
He helps me when I am weak, and he will catch
me when I fall.

Eat My Grits

The trip down south to the beach is an annual outing;
I study my maps for directions and precise routing.
My desire is to get tanned from my feet to my lips,
But what I love most is eating the Southern grits.

The first day at the beach will get me excited and pumped;
And too much shrimp and crab will probably get dumped.
I love sitting in the sand and exposing my northern hips,
But what I love most is eating those Southern grits

Early morning walkers seek seashells on the beach;

They all stopped to watch the sunrise in the
east.
Many look for the best spot on the beach to
sit,
But what I love most is a place that sells grits.

Volleyball is played and well-represented on the
shore;
Frisbee is another one and I'm sure there are
more.
Others sit under the umbrella with Jim Beam
for a nip,
But I'd rather be in a restaurant with a quart jar
of grits.

In addition to the ocean, there are hot tubs and
pools;
If you don't enjoy these amenities, you must be
a fool.
There are great pleasures down south to give
you a lift.
You can do all these things, but make sure you
have grits

Eating More Than You Need

Harsh words for junk food eaters are necessary and true.

The amount of candy you eat may inflate and obstruct my view.

Fat cells are growing, and you will be in an emotional slump;

Eating more than you need will only fill out your round rump.

The wider your bottom grows from all the candy and junk

Will tell you to decrease the size of your rear-end lump.

Fat cells are growing, and you will be in an emotional slump;

Eating more than you need will only fill out your round rump.

Eat two large pieces of cake but do not tell others a lie;
The additional calories are harmful, and you may slowly die.
Fat cells are growing, and you will be in an emotional slump;
Eating more than you need will only fill out your round rump.

Put down your fork and step away from the half-eaten cake;
Use an apple for dessert, or just put more salad on your plate.
Fat cells are growing, and you will be in an emotional slump;
Eating more than you need will only fill out your round rump.

If you are feeling weak and fear that others will call you fat;
Take a piece of candy to satisfy the cravings and hide like a rat.
Fat cells are growing, and you will be in an emotional slump;
Eating more than you need will only fill out your round rump.

If you feel well, with no worries, but have little pride;

Eat all you want in public till your butt is axe
handle wide.
Fat cells are growing, and you will be in an
emotional slump;
Eating more than you need will only fill out
your round rump.

Evildorth

The moon on holidays shines bright in
Evildorth each night;
Shadows from the coffin will cause sudden
nocturnal fright.

The coffin seems light without a body to make
it whole
Evildorth waits on a corpse like a mare waits
for the foal.

Men carry body bags while younger men carry
their axes.
They don't care about evidence that will reveal
the facts.

The group's leader points his finger to show the
group the way
To a mortal man who will be the victim, who
will soon have to pay.

The coffin causes single men to be troubled for
their lives;
And the future makes them wish they had
taken a wife.

Residents of Evildorth know of the nocturnal
evil work
But they will never interfere with these
malicious jerks.

Killing on holidays is the work of these men of
Evildorth
They murder travelers, especially on July the
Fourth.

Homicide on holidays is the plan for this
bailiwick
For many heads will be opened with an ax or
a pick.

When they arrive at the stump of a black cherry
tree
The leader stares at the others to decide if they
all agree.

Then a sharpened ax opens a victim's skull near
the stump;
And the wound reveals an artery spurting blood
like a pump.

The life of a stranger is taken like a piece of hanging fruit.
And he's hung in a tree as the crimson fluid soaks the roots.

These killers show no remorse since they think it is OK.
Death is common in Evildorth, especially on holidays.

This city holds a figment of imagination in one's mind,
Since many travelers are slain on holidays all the time.

Avoid Evildorth during holidays when the moon is bright.
I will not go to Evildorth, especially on New Year's Eve night.

Getting Into Trouble

The assessment of the eating habits of co-workers was delineated in a poem;
The text was left on lunchroom tables for others to read before going home.
I got into trouble because I fervently desired to put written words on paper;
But I cannot write poetry at work even when some employees show favor.

You can hold my feet to the fire when my job rating must be rescued;
But my playful attitude about the behinds of employees can't be excused.
I got into trouble because I fervently desired to put written words on paper;
But I cannot write poetry at work even when some employees show favor.

Some of my colleagues found the pranks a delight to break up the day.
But others were offended to see the truth portrayed this way.

I got into trouble because I fervently desired to
put written words on paper;
But I cannot write poetry at work even when
some employees show favor.

When cakes are delivered for parties and
employees pass them on to other jobs;
Don't criticize the eating habits of others who
often eat like slobs.
I got into trouble because I fervently desired to
put written words on paper;
But I cannot write poetry at work even when
some employees show favor.

Get a grip on life when you have nothing better
to do with your time;
Don't tell the boss I told you that eating cake
will make your butt wide.
I got into trouble because I fervently desired to
put written words on paper;
But I cannot write poetry at work even when
some employees show favor.

The revelation by the boss was a wake-up call
for my method of writing;
The poem about eating cake inspired me and I
found that it was very exciting.
I got into trouble because I fervently desired to
put written words on paper;
But I cannot write poetry at work even when
some employees show favor.

I promised I will never write a poem about the size of someone's butt;
I will not write to reveal that you will gain weight when the cake is cut.
I got into trouble because I fervently desired to put written words on paper;
But I cannot write poetry at work even when some employees show favor.

I must be circumspect when writing about the anatomy of people;
Those offended usually are overweight, but they are not sick or feeble.
I got into trouble because I fervently desired to put written words on paper;
But I cannot write poetry at work even when some employees show favor.

Good Genes

I have several medical conditions because of
my genes;
Due to my taste, I like peas and on other days
green beans.

There is a relationship between heart disease
and my dad;
The food that I've eaten at meals may make me
very sad.

Blood tests at the lab reveal that my total
cholesterol is high;
Will the results of the tests be altered if I get my
genes dried?

Studies show that genes with no shirt cause
sunburn in mice;
However, if your genes are too tight, make sure
you eat rice.

If I add bleach to my genes, will I turn into an
albino male?
Cut out the seat of the genes to make a mouse
without a tail.

Cut-off genes are contraindicated for people
who are short;
However, amputations are common in a cut-
off gene report.

Genes with a stain may cause controversy in a
public crowd;
And genes with multiple stains may cause the
odor to be foul.

Bell bottom genes indicate that ankles are filled
with fluid;
And genes that fray may show that a person is
worried.

Genes on a hanger routinely indicate the use of
hand gliders;
Leather jackets with genes are for those who
ride Harleys.

Make sure you know the tailor who will make
your genes fit;
Remember that God gives us at birth a brand-
new gene kit.

Greeting Card from Death

Death sent me a greeting card to reveal its plan for me;
The message was clear, but I could not fathom my destiny.

Plans for the future will be put on hold as I wait for Death;
Life is fading and I want more, but Death wants me as a guest.

Give me life, not the end of it, but Death will not grant my wish;
My plan won't be obscure for my family, nor my valued wish list.

I will leave my dreams with the memory of others I know.
And forget about a car, home, or even an expensive cell phone.

I must get ready for eternity since Death is calling my name;
I will forget about love, relationships, and a past that is full of shame.

Good-bye to all as I prepare to leave Earth for my eternal life;
Will it be full of blessings, love, or eternal misery and strife?

I know the answer to the question because I have trusted in God
So, I will be in Heaven with Jesus when I am laid under the sod.

Happiness is Optimism

H appiness in Life is measured by the positive experiences endured;
Success is increased by reversing negative experiences incurred.

Build sand forts on the beach and the tide will tear them down;
Don't worry about past failures; a smile is better than a frown.

Pessimists see the gloomy side of life when they make mistakes,
But optimists turn icy streets into opportunities to use ice skates.

Whining about what someone did to cause you pain,
Can make you lose happiness that may never be found again.

Sweep misery into the garbage disposal and make it go down the drain;
Let misery slowly leave your life to prevent you from being ashamed.

Life with Hannah

H is sweet lover's name is Hannah and
soon she'll be his beautiful bride.
As soon as the duty to the country is complete
and God willing, he does not die.

He is proud of his military service for it's the
obligation to his country he made;
It will soon be over, and he will return home
since his dues will have been paid.

He will make obligations to Hannah and plan
for a family and a new life;
It will be a pleasure to take off the uniform and
make this woman his wife.

Hannah's sweet voice gives him chills when he
thinks about the alluring past.
How much longer will the war cause this
separation from his love to last?

His longing for her endearing touch makes the
day seem much too long;
But he knows the waiting will pay off like the
melody of a love song.

The love they have is not circumscribed because
their relationship is a boon;
They endured much adversity, and he prayed
they would be together soon.

This bond they have for each other has taken
years to finally mature;
It is an ideal relationship, and he knows their
love will always endure.

He dreams of the years together with children,
a new career, and a home;
His love for Hannah includes years together
and grandkids on the roam.

But fate suddenly interrupted his life with an
Iraqi insurgent mortar round;
And the dreams with Hannah were lost at a
military funeral in his hometown.

Medical Hate

I hate cancer when it attacks my colon;
I hate fluid that makes me feel swollen.

I hate surgery when my tissue is cut;
I hate polyps that are found in my gut.

I hate fractures that cause broken bones;
I hate urinary problems that lead to stones.

I hate diabetes and I despise checks for glucose;
I hate medication and following an exact dose.

I hate renal problems with high potassium
levels;
I hate limiting bananas since it makes me a
devil.

I hate arthritis that restricts my walking and
bending;
I hate diarrhea in the morning with the toilet
pending.

I hate cataracts that reduce the ability to use
my sight;
I hate dysphasia when steaks are grilled just
right.

I hate pneumonia and other pulmonary
disorders;
I hate anal suppositories and following doctor's
orders.

I hate dermatitis and the lotion to apply to dry
skin;
I hate nasal discharge that drips time and again.

I hate heart attacks, especially congestive heart
failure;
I hate heart surgery in the hospital; it's like I'm
ruled by a jailer.

I hate leg amputations when I know they are
preventable;
I hate neuropathy in my feet when walking a
mile is amenable.

I dislike people who look for doctors and nurses
to hate;
But I love finding people who can make hate
dissipate.

My Church

(Put your place of worship in the blank)

At _____ the service begins with a handshake and hymn,
And our flamboyant pastor preaches on the enigma of sin.

"Make your life peaceful," he says, "and always seek out good;
Don't practice tomfoolery or act like a gullible inner-city hood".

Several at _____attend only to show off new clothes;
While an old, enervated man shuts his eyes and begins to dose.

Near the end of the service, the pastor emphasizes the plan,
And a young man walks to the alter waiving both of his hands.

When the service at _____concludes a woman waves a fan;
And many smiling parishioners will hug you and shake your hand.

A man behind me complains that his life is full of failure and loss;
A woman near him says "The pastor can help you understand the cost."

At _____ you can always find peace and hope for all of your life;
And forget your unscrupulous and regretful pain that causes strife.

_____ is where all God's children are welcome to come and pray;
The gracious Holy Spirit filled my life for yet another glorious day.

My Grief

My grief is ostensible in the eyes of the ordinary woman or man;
I cannot look at her photograph without it shaking in my hand.
Because of my mother's guidance, I feel more adept at basic math;
She proved to me early how to count change without a task.

I am saturated with depression about the end of her maternal plight;
My morose behavior is due to the absence of my mother's life.
I cannot fight the pressure that swells in my chest when I think of her;
The capricious thoughts of our relationship are as precious as myrrh.

Natural Web Site

While I was walking to my car late in the evening one day;
I noticed a scent in our pasture where we had just cut hay.

The aroma drew me nearer to the entrance of the barn
Where I first noticed the site that made me write this yarn.

In the wide doorway of the barn high in the right-hand corner
I noticed a small shiny spider that I knew must be a foreigner.

This little arachnid was weaving a web that was very precise;
And I noticed in the center a message the size of a speck of ice.

I got closer to reading the written words in the middle of the web;
And I saw minuscule white letters that were delineated in red.

The white letters spelled a website that I could not believe;
It read WWW.BARNSPIDER.COM but how could that be?

I was so amazed that I wanted to alert someone of this wonder;
I had to e-mail my friends and ask them about this blunder.

I turned on my PC quickly and opened my inbox for Outlook Express;
When I saw the most recent e-mail I received, I knew I needed a rest.

To my amazement, I had an e-mail from richmac@barnspider.com
I didn't want to open it because I was afraid, I was too far gone.

But I hurriedly clicked on the e-mail and read it slowly with fright;
The subtle message in this e-mail has entirely changed my life.

It began, "Hi RichMac, I noticed you peering
at my web at the barn;
I am a spider, and I am sending you an e-mail,
so don't buy the farm".

The message went on to inform me of the most
inimitable news;
"I spoke to your mother who told me she has
paid her life's dues;

She is no longer afraid of spiders because we are
products of GOD;
And she wanted me to tell you she was safe
with HIM, not just in the sod".

This spider was the messenger between me and
my dear mother;
And I got responses when seeking advice for
me, my sister, and my brother.

I noticed that when fall arrived, and the nights
became very cool;
There was no natural website or e-mail, and I
thought I was a fool.

Next year when the midday reached a high
temperature of eighty degrees
My eyes found again at the barn that
phenomenon which brought joy to me.

A natural website was erected by another barn
spider with a neat new web
And at once the e-mail began from the website
outlined in red.

I received no more information from my
mother, but I was not sad;
Because I began receiving information, advice,
and wisdom from my dad.

This has continued for years, and it makes me
so happy to know I'm secure;
Because I know the everlasting happiness of my
great family will endure.

Nature in the Evening

The wind from the ocean delivers its fresh
message to the sea oats on the shore;
They accept the words brought by the wind
and are constantly listening for more.

The sun has departed to make its journey in
preparation for another new day;
Men, nor women can intervene to make
changes because there is no other way.

The white surf lunges making the tide whip its
fingers against the sandy shore;
And the miles of beaches will receive the
immense waves like an open door.

The cumulous clouds that linger high in the
sky will hide the twinkling stars;
Just like the moon is absent as well as the planets
Venus, Mercury, and Mars.

The dew will fall later in the evening covering every plant and leaf with water.

All these great wonders of Nature are gifts from the blessed Heavenly Father.

Obese Woman

I love women, especially those who display
fervent personalities with wrath;
I look forward to my quiescent evenings after
walking along a dark path.
My obese wife seeks her mercenary ploy to
improve my daily habits.
The foible of her health is the absence of eating
vegetables like a rabbit.

The transitory women in my life have made
poignant statements to my peers;
They made me aware of the need to rid my life
of the abject hags for years.
Fellow colleges express concern regarding the
squalid appearance of the hogs;
And I considered drafting her demise by leading
her to the morass in the fog.

Her dress made a blatant statement with the
uncanny color in the seam.

Her ostensible size fooled my friends when she
stood near the ball team.
I was embarrassed by the amount of material
used to repair the hem.
But the adipose formed a blob that stretched
the tawdry lace over her skin.

The task of brushing the hair under her arms
was a nightmare last night;
She screamed when the tissue bled from the
bristles as sharp as a knife
I had no idea that the fat was pliant when the
brush lacerated her huge arm
I retorted quickly "Shut your mouth or I will
surely make you buy the farm".

Her unscrupulous principles make her flippant
when speaking to you or me.
I am melancholy when she uses her street jargon
and asks men for the fee.
She does not recognize the need for an urbane
relationship with other men.
She is not able to recognize the transgressions
when she takes part in sin.

Please help me leave her in the clandestine life
she has developed in time;
Sexual innuendoes always degrade her style of
flattery when she sips wine.

The nebulous excuses she makes regarding her diet are only a tirade each day
So, I will reject my life with her and show how she will learn to pay.

My ambiguous life with the queen of obesity has ended and she died in shame.
The tons of food she consumed each month led to an expunged life of pain.
I want to repudiate my life with that obese woman who embellished the truth.
A heavy ostentatious woman is gone, and I will trade her chocolates for fruit.

Obesity is Spelled F-A-T

A s a dietitian in West Virginia, I saw obesity increase each year,
So, I developed a run to help folks realize the size of their rear.

The campaign was an effort to increase awareness about being overweight
This Obesity Run permitted runners to run on highways throughout the state

I know a man who realizes his obesity particularly when his pants are split;
He drinks cola with doughnut holes and tries to trick me with his wit.

He is a congenial fellow with a good attitude, who tries to disguise his guilt,
But the adipose tissue that makes up his stomach is larger than a folded quilt.

He quickly grew a double chin from eating
McDonald's healthy meals of fun;
His cholesterol increased from weight, and he
smirked at the Obesity Run.

His wife is an oversized woman with robust
hips and tries to fake her size,
But the breadth of her rear cannot be hidden
whenever she looks into my eyes.

Her vigorous appetite grew, and she always
feasted till all the food was gone;
When she surreptitiously holds her abdomen,
it appears that she is hiding a fawn.

She laughed, pointed, and jeered as the runners
ran swiftly across the state,
And Diabetes suddenly knocked at her door to
reveal her hyperglycemic fate.

They don't want to work their hearts by being
active at the end of the day;
He likes triple servings of ice cream, and she
will not give up the bags of Lays.

He insisted that I not call him or offer a solution
to remedy his obtuse physique,
But his wife will need insulin for her sugar,
especially for the after-meal peaks.

A dinner consisting of a plate heaped with fries
will provide quantities of fat;
Scientific research completed in all medical
schools will explain the origin of that.

Unfortunately, they don't care that their navels
have grown to the size of a peach!
They need to get up, stretch their legs, and walk
at the mall or on the beach.

Pleasures of the Seashore

The warmth of the sun makes me lazy
while I sit on the beach and write;
The waves pound the shore to display their
force and ferocious might.

Dolphins are visible within one hundred yards
of bathers on the shore;
Men and women retrieve their cameras
snapping photos and want more.

Children dig in the sand while their fathers
assist with the engineering task;
Mothers help their children and usually do not
even have to be asked.

The surf provides pleasure and excitement as it
curls viciously into the sand;
This is the force of Mother Nature as she slaps
the sea with her giant hand.

The tide moves closer to claim the chairs we
positioned earlier in the morning;
By mid-day, the silent water creeps up to our
toes with very little warning.

In the sky, Navy jets practice maneuvers flying
as fast as the speed of sound;
It makes me so proud to be an American
whether I'm at home or in this town.

The sun delivers rays of ultraviolet penetrating
deep into my exposed skin;
I hope my sunscreen is effective so I can return
to enjoy the seashore again.

Rosa's Mother

O nce near noon while the sun shone bright
in the sky;
My stomach was yearning for a big piece of
Rosa's pie.

We were together last night, and we rolled in
the hay;
Rosa's mother nearly caught us, but I was ready
to pay.

She is nineteen but she is treated like she is
nearly nine;
The better I get to know her she will finally be
mine.

Rosa is a cook at the restaurant and her specialty
is pie;
I can eat a whole one but please don't make me
tell a lie.

So, I went to the restaurant to get my lunch for
the road;
I had to deal with Rosa's mother who looked
like a toad.

I asked for beef, lettuce, cheese, and a load of
napkins;
At that time, I was following the diet of Dr.
Atkins.

When the order came out with the cheese on
the side,
A piece of pie had been added by my future
bride.

Her mother was suspicious, and she had a look
of doubt;
She couldn't believe that little Rosa had figured
it out.

We had worked on a special signal when I came
to eat;
She would add pie when a customer requested
only meat.

This worked in the meantime, but her mother
caught on,
Especially when I was found in Rosa's bedroom
at dawn.

Her mother threw a fit and she screamed loudly;
There was nothing I could do but act like I was proud.

I told her I loved Rosa and there was nothing she could do;
It appeared in the meantime she was ready to file a lawsuit.

But when she saw me hand Rosa the two-carat diamond ring;
She had a change in demeanor, and I thought she would sing.

That was years ago and now Wanda is my mother-in-law;
Her daughter Rosa is the mother of my precious son Paul.

Rosa quit cooking and assisted me with finishing law school;
I use a laptop in the courtroom and the law books are my tools.

I had years of experience with domestic violence-related cases;
My job was worthwhile for Rosa, Paul, and other little faces.

Yes, we had five more children and Wanda
offered a helping hand;
She watched them when Rosa traveled with me
to a trial in Spokane.

Wanda was the caretaker of our children when
Rosa and I went away;
These trips were more frequent, and Wanda
related "I request to be paid".

She brought to me receipts from expenses that
were dated for years;
She quickly got my attention, but Rosa could
not hold back her tears.

"Mother", Rosa said, "Why are you waiting till
now to bring this out?
Wanda began speaking softly and then suddenly
she started to shout.

"I did nothing but wait on tables when you
cooked and baked pies;
You saw your husband in the restaurant, and
you flashed your eyes".

"He took you to your bedroom and you all had
your fun all night,
But your poor mother paid the bills and that
was a sorry sight.

I have only social security and what I make
from cleaning homes,
And you two are always on trips driving, flying,
and on the roam.

Well, I've had it to her as she raised her hand to
just below her chin;
I'm going to court to sue you for what you owe
me, and I will win.

I asked her to tell me what the amount was she
wished to be paid
Because as a defendant against my wife's mother
was not the way.

"Eighty-five thousand includes all the expenses
as well as the interest;
Two hundred per hour is the fee calculated by
my accountant Vincent.

We settled the case instead of going to trial and
embarrassing our family;
We now get along well since my wife's
stepmother's name is Tammy.

THE HOE

While driving to my job I noticed a hoe along the road
She was dressed in a split leather skirt and a dirty coat.
I liked the way she looked so I found some space in the trunk
But placing the hoe in my car was like hauling junk.

She objected to the bumpy ride and decided to call the police
The complaint the cops made was failing to pay her fee.
"I have a hoe in the trunk of my car," I told the Police Captain
"I thought I might take the hoe home and plan for some action".

The captain became irritated and decided to send me to jail;

He laughed and pointed his finger, and it made me yell.
I told the jailer I got caught with a hoe in the trunk of my car;
He laughed so loud that I swore an oath like a sailor in a bar.

"Why would you stoop so low to pick up a hoe off the street"?
"There are plenty of girls available for a young man to meet".
I could not understand the reasoning of the young jailer man
He twisted things around so badly that I took off my wedding band.

"What do you mean?" I asked not understanding his thoughts,
"How can you confuse a gardening tool with a young sexy fox?"
"A gardening tool?" the jailer asked not believing what I said;
"You say it is a garden tool and I think you will take her to bed".

"The judge will get your case tomorrow and you can tell the truth;
But remember that the Judge's daughter is the captain's wife Ruth"

I knew it would be bad when I swore tomorrow and told this story:
"I found a hoe beside the road to help weed my morning glories".

That's the truth and I will stick to that no matter how bad it looks
The captain will beguile the truth while the judge refers to books.
I made a mistake by picking up a hoe and I will not do it again
With these terrible odds against my case, how will I ever win?"

In the morning at seven-thirty, the judge sat on the bench
He picked up the docket and called the first name "Joe Wrench".
I quickly approached the judge and said, "It's me, your honor."
"Joe", he said, "you picked up a hoe" and I knew I was a goner.

"The captain said he saw a hoe in your trunk, so what is your plea"?
I knew that this family legal affair was not going to be good for me.
"Your Honor, tools are in my blood just like my name is Wrench,

So, I stopped to pick up another tool and that is how I will finish".

This tool case was set for trial, and I asked for some legal advice
So, the lawyer appointed was Mr. Socket and he was nice
"We tools have to stick together", Mr. Socket told me that night;
He convinced me I was telling the truth, adding that I was right.

The court started the next morning with the same judge on the case.
My lawyer gave the tool story, and he convinced the judge to wait.
"Other witnesses have to be called your honor to set my client free".
An assortment of tools will provide evidence to certainly help me.

A one month of continuance was given by the vindictive circuit judge
He could not be bribed with a stack of twenties or even a pan of fudge.
My counselor met with three tools and planned a meeting in a week;
The first tool was a shovel with a handle made from shiny Indian teak.

Mr. Shovel said he knew the hoe but had no
knowledge about that night
I knew that my luck was bad but there was no
earthly reason to fright
The other tool was Mrs. Rake and I've known
her for twenty years;
I met her after college when I dated her sister
who is quite dear.

Mrs. Rake told my lawyer she saw the hoe that
night at nearly nine;
The more she talked it seemed the acquittal
would certainly be mine.
The relationship between Mrs. Rake and the
hoe sealed my arrest
It leads me to understand the Police Captain
was nothing but a pest.

The third tool was Pick, a man who knows how
to select his friends
The counselor asked him several times about
his inequities and sins.
It was apparent to me quickly that Mr. Pick
had no information to offer
We got his address and bid him farewell since
he had no credible proffer.

I told my lawyer he was only draining from me
the money I had paid;

I decided to hire a new law firm whose
controlling partner is Mr. Spade.
The reason for sticking with tools when the
future is not looking bright
Is what I need from my experience to keep
myself out of a dirty fight.

Mr. Spade convinced me to lay myself at the
mercy of the court.
He said I would come out ahead if I just pled
guilty to the tort.
I know now he is right because as a sharp tool
I am effective;
It is better to get sharpened than to live a lie
and be deceptive.

The moral of this story will not be forgotten as
I think of the past;
Picking up a hoe while I am married will not
enable a marriage to last
Tools are for physical labor, and they assist men
with laborious jobs.
But hoes are for men with bad intentions who
often get robbed.

Wanda's Heart

H er heart is beating just a little slow;
　　She could tell by the pain in the chest, you know.

Her surgeon found lesions in two arteries of the heart,

And plans are underway to get her back to K-Mart.

She went to the Cath lab for a balloon and a stint,

But they found a blocked one in the artery that was bent.

Wanda is now waiting for a CABG next week;

The knowledge of the medical staff is what we will seek.

The hospital does surgeries on thousands of hearts.

And we hope medical teams do all their part.

We love our Wanda, and we want her to live

To a ripe old age of 90 helping others who give.

Wanda's heart is a big one and it is full of love;

We pray that His hand will be on her chest from Heaven above...

TIME

I love to know what time it is. I catch myself looking at the clock in the middle of the night on my nightstand. The red numbers tell me the time. I must know what time it is. Why? I guess I am just a time guy. For my convenience I prefer my timepieces to be in military time. As a friend of mine used to say, "There's no doubt in my military mind". The small timing device on my electronic toothbrush keeps me looking at how much time has elapsed when I brush my teeth each day. I intensely want to recognize how much time is spent when I complete this chore.

Time for God is immeasurable. According to 2 Peter Chapter 3 verse 8: "But, beloved do not forget this one thing, that with the Lord one day is as a thousand years and a thousand years as one day."

God is eternal, but we measure time by day and night. When the earth has revolved one time on its axis one day has passed. In the Bible in the book of Revelation chapter 22 verse 5, it says: "There should be no night there: They need no lamp nor no light of the sun, for the Lord God gives them light. And they shall reign forever and ever."

With that in mind there will not be any need for a clock or watch in Heaven for all the time it is the same. When Jesus ascended to heaven from earth the disciples watched him go up. The book of Acts Chapter 1 verses 10 and 11 says: "And while they looked steadfastly toward heaven as He went up, behold, two men stood by them in white apparel, who also said, "Men of Galilee why do you stand gazing up into heaven? This same Jesus, who was taken up from you into heaven, will also come in like manner as you saw Him go into heaven."
These men were probably angels, and I wonder if they had some insight as to when Jesus would be returning to earth. It sounded like they were characterizing time to the disciples. He went to heaven, but will He be back next week, or next year, or in 100 years, or 1000 years? They may not see time as we humans see time.

Humans are so disciplined to time. What time is my appointment next Tuesday with my doctor? What time is my favorite episode of the Andy Griffith Show going to be broadcast on television? What time does the Super Bowl begin?

I get asked about time. What time do you wish to be here for your haircut next week? And what day? My doctor only sees patients on Mondays. Oh my, I'll be late for work. I need to be on time because I have been late before, and I got warned when I was late the last time. The boss said "Next time, and you will be gone! "

I pray to God every day and that is a reference to time. I always praise God as I pray before I eat a meal or when I spend 15 minutes or 30 minutes in prayer to God. When I spend time in God's word it means I am with God in spirit. I listen to God through his Word in the Bible.

Some time ago I wrote notes in the composition book I am using now. I wrote a group of statements. I do not know when they were written.

Jesus the Blesser

To find blessings from Jesus don't listen to crowds but listen to the Savior.

Ask: What does Jesus say? Focus on your faith. Do focus on faith in him

Ask what He can do for you.

Find your amazing grace in Jesus.

I was talking to my brother and sister this morning about an event my brother and I participated in about 30 years ago in Belle Glade, Florida where our parents lived. The subject came up because the 2021 Black Gold Jubilee will be April 17, 2021. Our parents lived in a huge mobile trailer parked at a camping lot in Belle Glade near Lake Okeechobee. The black gold is the dirt the community uses in growing so many vegetables and sugarcane and the festival includes a 5K/10K walk/run. My brother and I ran in the race and because of my age, I received a third-place award for the running event. This all has to do with time. The questions I asked were:

What time is the run?

What day and time do my flight leave to travel to Florida?

What time do we have to leave to get to the start of the run?

I am annoyed that my online church bulletin does not have a date. When I look at the bulletin, I'll look first for the date. Is there anything wrong with that?

The Time Machine movies always have intrigued me. To have the power and knowledge of time travel is amazing. The news reporting about a person who is in a coma or someone who has been separated from society for several years and learns of new inventions that we have had at our disposal for use for years is also captivating.

When I turn on my smartphone, I like looking at the date and time. There is so much more time that has passed. How much more time till my federal tax payment is due? How much time till lunch or dinner? Does my stomach have an internal clock that tells me when to eat? I am starting to get hungry. It must be near 11:00 AM.

At the beginning of time when God created the heavens and the earth according to Genesis chapter 1 verse 26: "Then God said, "let us make man in Our image, according to Our likeness; let them have dominion over the fish of the sea over the birds of the air and the cattle, over every creeping thing that creeps on the earth."

Time is referenced in the Bible.

Nehemiah Chapter 1 Verses one and two: The words of Nehemiah the son of Hachaliah. It came to pass in the month of Chislev, in the twentieth year, as I was in Shushan the citadel, that Hanani one of my brethren came with men from Judah; and I asked them concerning the Jews who had escaped, who had survived the captivity, and of Jerusalem.

According to www.thefreedictionary.com Chislev means the third month of the semi-year in the ninth month of the ecclesiastical year in the Jewish year. (Judaism) The calendar used by the Jews; dates from 3761 BC (the assumed date of the creation of the world) and is adjusted to the solar year by periodic sleep years.

From the Bible in the Book of Ezra Chapter 1 and the first part of verse 1: "Now in the first year of Cyrus king of Persia, that word of the Lord by the mouth of Jeremiah might be fulfilled, the Lord stirred up the spirit of Cyrus king of Persia..."

According to a Google search, Cyrus the Great of Persia died in 530 BC.

It is difficult to embrace the conception that Jesus, the son of God was with God the Father before the beginning of time and present in human form on earth thousands of years later.

The book of John chapter 17 verse 24 reads: "Father, I desire that they also whom You gave Me may be with Me where I am, that they may behold My glory which You have given Me; for You loved Me before the foundation of the world."

There have been many things written about time and some are quite electrifying.

Leo Tolstoy wrote in War and Peace, "The two most powerful warriors are patience and time."

We have all heard that "Time is money" as quoted by Benjamin Franklin. He also said, "Lost time is never found again."
Charles Dickens' epic novel A Tale of Two Cities begins with "It was the best of times, it was the worst of times, it was the age of wisdom, it was the age of foolishness, it was the epoch of belief, it was the epoch of incredulity; it was the season of light, it was the season of

darkness, it was the spring of hope, it was the winter of despair, we had everything before us, we had nothing before us, we were all going to Heaven, we were all going the other way-in short, the period was so far like the present period, that some of its noisiest authorities insisted on its being received, for good or evil, in the superlative degree of comparison only. My battery-operated toothbrush has a clock on the device that keeps track of the amount of time the toothbrush is used for brushing. Every thirty seconds the handle of the brush vibrates informing the user of the 30-second interval and time to change which part of the mouth to be cleaned. I catch myself looking at my watch to find out when the toothbrush's next buzzing lull will occur.

Matthew 24 verse 36 reads "But of that day and hour no one knows, not even the angels of heaven but My father only."

In William Shakespeare's play The Merry Wives of Windsor he quoted, "Better three hours too soon than a minute too late."

Theophrastus the Greek scholar said, "Time is the most valuable thing a man can spend."

Pericles the influential ancient Greek stated, "Time is the wisest counselor of all."

Stephen Covey in his monumental bestselling book, The Seven Habits of Highly Effective People wrote "The key is not spending time but investing in it.

In chapter 21 of The Little Prince Antione de Saint-Exupery the words are written "It is the time you have wasted for your rose that makes your rose so important."

Oscar Wilde wrote "Punctuality is the Thief of Time", in his 1890 novel, The Picture of Dorian Gray. The meaning of the quote is that when you amuse someone else by being punctual you are allowing the person to steal your precious time.

In 1965, the Rock group The Byrd's released their song Turn Turn Turn. The lyrics primarily came from the book of Ecclesiastes Chapter 3 written by King Solomon and inspired by God. It refers to a season and a time for every matter under heaven. A time to be born and a time to die.

Warren Wiersbe writes in The Bible Exposition and Commentary of the Old Testament

<u>Wisdom and Proverbs</u> (Job through Song of Solomon) published in 2004. "Psalm 139:13-16 states that God so wove us in the womb that our genetic structure is perfect for the work He has prepared for us to do.

It is also written in Ecclesiastes Chapter 3 that there is a time to kill and a time to heal;
 a time to break down and a time to build up;
a time to weep and a time to laugh;
a time to mourn and a time to dance;
a time to cast away stones and a time to gather stones;
a time to mourn and a time to dance;
a time to embrace a time to refrain from embracing;
a time to gain; a time to lose;
a time to keep; and a time to throw away;
a time to tear and a time to sew;
a time to keep silent and a time to speak;
a time to love and a time to hate;
a time for war and a time for peace.

The discussion of sleep time enters the picture because we all need to rest. How much time do I sleep compared to your sleep time? I usually get about 9 1/2 to 10 hours of sleep per night. That probably sounds like too much compared to others. I have gotten used to going to bed at approximately 9 o'clock in the evening and arising at about 6:30 in the morning.

Medications are available by prescription and non-prescription to aid in sleeping. I have been very blessed by God Almighty that I can sleep on my own and I don't need sleep slumber aids. People may go to sleep at night or some other time in the day thinking of a stressful issue they will have to deal with after the sleep period and it may affect their sleeping traits.
Questions often come up in conversation like, "Did you get a restful night's sleep?"

According to the Principles of Anatomy and Physiology 7th edition by authors Gerald J Tortora and Sandra Reynolds Grabowski, humans sleep and are awake in a consistent 24-hour cycle called circadian rhythm. When the brain is aroused or awakened it is in a state of readiness and able to react consciously to various stimuli. Neural fatigue proceeds with sleep and the signs of fatigue disappear after sleep; therefore, fatigue is apparently one cause of sleep.

Will you have time to get what you want to do in a day? There are many publications on time management. What about time sharing as it relates to real estate? Participants use the property for vacation time or sometimes folks share the use of the facility.

How much time am I spending writing this manuscript? How important is my time in writing this published article? The hope of attracting others to read the manuscript after it is published is an honor.

Time is precious. Please use it wisely.

FALLING FECES

Catastrophe One

I was diagnosed with myelodysplastic syndrome in the spring of 2014 after many physician appointments, including blood tests bone marrow biopsies, and finally a stem cell transplant. Most of the medical visits were at the Moffitt Cancer Center in Tampa, Florida in the fall of 2014 where I received donated stem cells from my brother who was a perfect match for me. One of the major side effects of the transplant was gastrointestinal (GI) abnormalities due to chemotherapy for the destruction of my stem cells. Through the weeks of post-transplant recovery and inheriting a new bone marrow system, I experienced bouts of diarrhea, nausea, vomiting, and constipation. Often this was the result of my nearly twenty prescribed medications, but with careful administration of the drugs, timing, and dose-dependent changes, the GI abnormalities became less severe. There were fewer days of diarrhea and more solid stools reappeared. This was preceded by three days of no bowel movements from one of my medications that has a side effect of constipation. To address the lack of stools, I consumed prunes, and bran muffins and ate Fiber One bars, and finally, at the beginning of the third day,

I felt pressure in my lower intestinal area and had a much-needed bowel movement. This was followed by an added smaller bowel movement later that morning.

On day 22 (twenty-two days after the transplant) in 2014 in the afternoon, my sister and I found a lovely bucolic park for walking and absorbing nature in Hillsborough County Florida just across the highway from our hotel called Lettuce Lake Park. The reptile and bird populations are so impressive to hikers as well as the hardwood swamp forest. We had such a good time walking and taking photos with our smartphones. We had arrived 45 minutes before the park closed so we had only a small amount of time to take in the 240-acre park. During the walk back to our vehicle, the urge to defecate suddenly occurred and we looked for a toilet. The urge continued and I was unable to restrain the natural flow of feces from my body. I walked faster and this behavior caused a small piece of excrement to roll down my leg settling between my right ankle and the top of my New Balance walking shoe. I stopped and pointed out to my sister the embarrassing sight that immediately began to exude a horrible odor, but she thought I was shaking a leaf off my shoe when I shook my leg causing the small piece of manure to be flung to the middle of the concrete sidewalk we were walking on. We laughed and continued to walk to the toilet, and I was able to finish relieving myself. It was a surreal experience.

Catastrophe TWO

T he measurement of my Pulmonary Function tests between August 2017 and November 2017 of the Total Lung Capacity (TLC) and the Forced Vital Capacity (FVC} decreased significantly. The TLC was down 16.5 percent and the FVC was down 19 percent. What if anything does air moving through the body have to do with feces? Wait and I will tell you.

It was after 0730 when I replaced the Crocs I was wearing with the size 12 New Balance 1080 running shoes. These were placed on my feet covered with black compression knee-high stockings because of the swelling I was experiencing in my lower legs and ankles. On my upper body was a dark long-sleeved shirt to cover my arms from the sunshine that would soon be radiating. My head was garnished with a very wide-brim hat to protect my neck, face, and head from the rays of the Florida sunshine. I was wear-ing a pair of green athletic shorts that sagged down to the top of the black compression hosiery.

I began walking along the street where my brother lives, passing home after home and stirring the attention of barking dogs looking out windows and glass storm doors. My determination was to walk the one-and-one-half miles to the CVS Pharmacy at the intersection of Darlington Road and U.S. Route 19 in Holiday, Florida, and back for about three miles. After walking about one-quarter of a mile during the trek I developed some minor pain in my right lower back. I thought of taking an aspirin or some other over-the-counter medication holding acetylsalicylic acid, but the longer I walked the pain receded. When I reached the halfway point at the CVS store, I made the circle around the building and began the walk back to my destination. Suddenly when I was three-fourths complete, I felt movement in my bowels and a need to get to the toilet quickly. That made me walk faster to complete the walk, but it also hastened the need to defecate. When the point of no return approached, I placed my left hand over the rear of my shorts and suddenly realized that I was not wearing any underwater and the feces began teetering out of my body in the form of chocolate pudding. I knew the volume of the excrement was voluminous since dung was dropping down the legs of my shorts and down the black compression socks to the back of my shoes. When I returned my hand from holding the back of my shorts, I noticed that my fingers were brown and covered in what was seeping through my shorts. I knew that if I passed anyone in their yard, they would be able to see a very boisterous dark stain on my backside. I was so embarrassed as I continued walking. When I reached my destination, I went directly to the water hose at the side of the house and removed my shoes so I could wash the feces from the back and sides of the shoes. I had to use so much water my stocking feet were standing in water. When I completed that task, I slowly entered the house, went to the area where I sleep and retrieved two disposable towels. One was placed on the floor to catch any remaining particles of feces that might fall from my rectum as well as the shorts that I dropped to the floor. The other was placed on the seat of the chair to prevent any stain on the chair. Next, I had to remove the wet compression socks which are just about as impractical to remove as walking on the moon. It took several agonizing minutes to get the socks off and get as quickly as possible to the shower to get cleaned up. Afterward, I placed the pads and the shorts in the trash can outside.

All in all, it was a very unforgettable walk. It was not pleasant, but now that it is over, I can grin a little.

Catastrophe Three

I learned after the stem cell transplant; I had a chance of acquiring GRAFT versus HOST DISEASE (GVHD). It is a condition that 30 to 60 percent of transplanted patients may acquire. This condition is caused by the transplanted stem cells rejecting the body or hosting the new cells residing, often causing other maladies to exist. I did contract GVHD, and I picked up scleroderma and dry eyes. The scleroderma, a connective tissue disease involves thickening and tightening of the skin. In my specific condition, the parts of the body that were affected were the abdomen, arms, and legs. It was almost impossible for me to bend forward to pick up items on the floor and dress and undress myself. It was a nightmare to live with.

I was taking multiple medications while recovering from the transplant and dealing with scleroderma causing frequent bowel movements. Some of the bowel movements were classical causing some very embarrassing catastrophic events. One episode occurred while I was at an appointment at the cancer center. After having an EKG, I was told to wait in the exam room for the results of the procedure. While waiting, I had a sudden urge to defecate so I quickly walked to the restroom to take care of my business. As I was locking the door on the inside of the restroom a stool I could not control was gathered in my bowels and ended up in my underwear. That was followed by a second and third stool that traveled past my briefs and lodged in the leg of my jogger scrub pants with tight legs.

Part of another stool found its way down into my left compression stocking. I sat on the toilet and tried removing my shoes to undress and remove the feces from my clothing. While doing so, part of one of the stools that had lodged in my scrub pants fell into my left shoe and onto the floor of the bathroom in front of the commode. It was like having a dreadful dream. The whole process for a person with scleroderma took nearly forty-five minutes and while all this was happening there were five attempts by people trying to get into the toilet.

It was not a pleasant experience.

THE GREAT EVENT

No one had the foresight to know about the great event that happened after the COVID-19 pandemic in the first quarter of the year 2020. The pandemic was one of many tragedies in this world. In the United States, all 50 states were under a disaster declaration by the U.S. government. The unemployment rate in late March 2020 was near 18% with some economists reporting anecdotally that the current unemployment rate would mimic the rate after the great depression in 1933 at almost 25%. Businesses were shut down to discourage people from gathering in large groups to prevent the spread of the virus. Likewise, theaters, restaurants, parlors, shopping malls, hair salons, schools, colleges and universities, gymnasiums, and dry cleaners were all closed to discourage people from gathering and promoting the coronavirus.

The virus tore the world apart since nearly all travel ceased and almost all people worldwide were remanded to their homes. An illuminated sign on an interstate highway read "essential travel only." The most frequented businesses were grocery stores and pharmacies. The retired people who were getting paid from pensions, annuities, and Social Security in the U.S. were only annoyed by the change in business as usual, but folks who were paid hourly wages struggled to make ends meet during the virus pandemic. People were made aware of the death toll resulting from the pandemic via television, radio, newspapers, and phone and device applications. According to the United States Centers for Disease Control and Prevention, about 500 million people worldwide were infected by the 1918 influenza epidemic. A little over one million people in the United States died from the pandemic.

The resounding message during the coronavirus pandemic was to stay at home, keep six feet from others, and wear a mask so you do not cause others to become infected with the virus. It was amazing that many people who were asymptomatic unknowingly infected others.

This made me think of the time after my stem cell transplant when I was so immune suppressed that I became vulnerable to others who might be infected with influenza, a cold, or other bacterial or viral diseases. My immune system was dismal, and I had to wear a mask and take many antibiotics including immune suppressant drugs. For a period after the hospitalization for the transplant, I had to live at a safe and approved location that was near the cancer center. My choice was a Residence Inn. The room had to be cleaned often, and the air filters had to be changed regularly to ensure that there was fresh airflow for the room. During my stay there I exhibited flu-like symptoms with a fever, sneezing, and a sore throat. My nose was swabbed, and it was confirmed that I did have the influenza virus. When my doctor found out about my condition he was infuriated and directed someone from the cancer center to call the hotel to find out how the flu virus was introduced to me. It was decided that a member of the cleaning staff had contracted the flu and spread it to me and others. The Residence Inn nearly lost approval of the cancer center to house transplant patients.

The loss of life was on the mind of all people and those in all walks of life saluted the heroes in the healthcare industry who were in contact with COVID-19 patients all day. Likewise, other heroes like first responders, firefighters, law-enforcement officers, paramedics, and EMS personnel were hailed but this was extended to everyone who had to work with people in public. Additionally, restaurant and fast-food personnel who risked their lives every day to provide food to the public were included. These actions slightly supported their livelihood. One of the greatest locations hard hit by the coronavirus in the United States was New York and many people watched day after day the television broadcast of the governor of New York providing statistics on the various outcomes Governors of many states were updating their citizens on the current news of the virus as well. The President of the United States held a coronavirus update each day to inform Americans of the battle with the virus and how the U S was combating the invisible enemy

THEN IT HAPPENED. The rapture of the church happened in the twinkling of an eye. The new heroes were all gone now. These were the faith-based church pastors and Christians who proclaimed their faith and led those who were not Christians to the Lord. This return of Jesus happened about two weeks ago, and I am writing this from heaven. I know that governments on Earth are struggling to understand how and why so many humans suddenly disappeared from the Earth. People remembered what evangelists Billy Graham, David Jerimiah, and others had said about the need to come to Christ for eternal life and how Jesus was going to be coming back to take the Christians to heaven. No one on earth was concerned any longer about the COVID-19 virus. The healthcare industry suffered greatly since many of the health maintenance workers had left Earth and were in heaven.

When Christ had returned to take all those who believed in him to heaven the entire earth fell apart. There were hundreds of airline flights that crashed on Earth and millions of people were killed in automobile accidents all over the Earth when the cars the Christians were driving careened off bridges and crashed into embankments and hillsides. The world news agencies remarked hour after hour what happened. Citizens from all over the world were challenged to tell what they believed happened two weeks ago. People remarked how dissimilar their lives were now. Others remarked that they remembered the words of their loved ones and friends who were no longer with them and told the stories of going to heaven and the need to trust in Jesus. One man was heard saying to a friend, "Wow, and I thought the confusion, mistrust, and hopelessness was bad when that virus came on the earth." There were so many members of the United States Senate and House of Representatives and the Supreme Court to suddenly leave. It left the United States in a quandary to fulfill its mission to provide needed funding and services to the citizens of the country.

It reminded me of a Netflix series titled "Designated Survivor" that portrayed the loss of the president of the United States, all his cabinet members except one, and nearly all the members of Congress and the Supreme Court. Many other countries on Earth succumbed to this predicament too. Many people looked for someone to blame. It was a sad time for those remaining on earth.

I am so joyous that I left the earth with all my hardships, and I now live with Jesus. I have seen my parents and grandparents as well as many friends who died many years ago. It is wonderful to see with my own eyes what was only read previously in God's word.

Just as the Disciple John described in the Bible in chapter 22 of the book of Revelation there is great tasting fruit from trees that are in the middle of the street and on each side of the river. These fruit trees bear 12 fruits every month. I love being here. It is remarkable. Food is plentiful here. The streets are made of gold, and it has been amazing to walk up to the throne of God and praise him in person. The Old Testament prophets like Moses, David, Solomon, and Paul are here and I sure like talking to them. Job is such a good man to speak to.

I know I should feel sorry for those left behind, but they were warned over and over. My friend told me about a coworker who got sick and, in a few days, died. The friend thought about all the times when in conversation with the sick man he just did not bring up the conversation about Jesus and the need to confess his sins and be saved, but he was dead in a few days.

All that is in the past.

I thought about my cat Zeke when he went outside. When all was well, he came back into the house very slowly. Sometimes he entered so slowly that I thought and even sometimes said to the cat "Will you hurry up and get in here. Stop wasting energy," but when he was outside and there was some abnormal sound or bark from a strange dog he raced in the house with no encouragement. And then there were those times when he was terrified of something outside, and he meowed and meowed so loud he could be heard through the door. During those times he charged into the house and went to one of his hiding places. My point is that I wished that I had behaved like the cat when it was terrified and told so many more people about the need to trust Jesus as their Savior so they would be with me in heaven.

I thought about this matter of pets many years ago and wondered what would happen to my pets after the rapture when my wife and I were suddenly taken away. I used this as a tool to convince others of the need to turn to Christ and be safe to prevent them from going to hell. There were some who were adamant about not wanting to discuss the need to trust in Jesus. I worked out a deal with one man who laughingly told me he would take care of my cats and dog when I was suddenly removed from the earth. I gave him my alarm code to get into the house and he knows how much when and where to feed Lindsey, the dog, Zeke, and our two new black kittens. There was too much sadness on earth as the bible described, but I am in heaven now and there is nothing but peace and happiness. There is no need for the police, hospitals, or anything related to the tragedies on Earth.

In the second letter the Apostle Paul composed to Timothy, he wrote "that the last days perilous times will come."

The Disciple Matthew quoted what Jesus said, "And you will hear of wars and rumors of wars. See that you are not troubled; for all these things must come to pass, but the end is not yet. For nation will rise against nation and kingdom against kingdom. And there will be famines and pestilences and earthquakes in various places."

In the first letter to the Church in Thessalonica, Chapter 4, the Apostle Paul wrote "For the Lord Himself will descend from Heaven with a shout, with the voice of an archangel, and with the trumpet of God. And the dead in Christ will rise first."

Yes, the bodies in the cemeteries arose first and met their spirits. The spirits of my mother and father were joined at the time of the rapture. That was impressive. Those who were never in tune with the Father God or His son Jesus will rise after one thousand years on earth and then go to hell.

Again, the Apostle Paul wrote in his second letter to the Church in Thessalonica in Chapter Two "Let no one deceive you by any means; for that day will not come unless the falling away comes first, and the man of sin is revealed, the son of perdition, who opposes and exalts himself above all that is called God or that is worshiped, so that he sits as God in the temple God, showing that he is God.

In the bible, I know from my earlier studies of the seven years of turmoil on earth when Satan, the antichrist, and the false prophet have their time to cause as much havoc, death, and destruction as they can. When I was living on earth, I always ended my emails with "If you miss the rapture, don't take the Mark of the beast. "The beast or antichrist will demand that everyone left on earth after the rapture display on their hand or forehead the mark (666) to buy food or other essentials and conduct any business. The reason for this will be to show allegiance to the antichrist and Satan. But after seven years, the antichrist and false prophet will be sent to hell or the fiery furnace for eternity. Satan however will be locked down in hell for 1000 years. I know it will be wonderful to return to earth after these seven horrible years and be in the presence of Jesus when He will be king of the world. I hope you are ready for that.

Praise God.

The Flying Phone

Gene, my brother, traveled to Sam's Club to buy groceries and other household items. During the trip home he called me just to chit-chat and to get caught up on whatever was happening During the trip home, he realized that he was nearly out of gas and decided to return to Sam's Club to fill up. Gene had access to both the Bluetooth headphones clipped to his ear as well as the Bluetooth in the car When he was in the car he listened to and spoke via the car Bluetooth, but when he was out of the car getting gas, he used the Bluetooth connected to his ear. After filling up he left the gas pump and headed home As we continued our conversation, I heard a small, strange sound and then a subsequent louder sound I asked Gene if he was OK, but I got no response

I kept asking, "Gene are you OK?" There was no response, but I could hear sounds from the phone, but no human sound Suddenly I noticed on my smartphone another call that was from Gene's company phone

I answered the call and Gene said "I've lost my phone. I left it on the top of my car when I was getting gas and it slid off when I drove away. I'm sure it's in a million pieces. I'm going to go back and look for it. I'll call you back from my company phone if I find my phone."

"Wait", I told him. "I can hear sounds from the phone that slid off the car. It must be OK. It sounds like traffic is passing by."

We ended the conversation, and I could still hear sounds from the phone that slid off the roof of the car.

Suddenly a voice said, "Look, a cell phone".

Whose name or number is on the screen of the phone? "A second voice asked.

The first voice said, "It is RichMac".

At that point, I yelled "Hey, it's my brother's phone that slid off the roof of his car when he was driving, and he was looking for it. Where are you? I will tell him where you are found."

"I'm on US 19 in Holiday, Florida at Trouble Creek Road." The voice said.

"OK, please stay there along the road and I'll call my brother on his company phone and tell him where you are. What are you wearing, what is your name so I can tell him? He is driving a silver 2012 Toyota Prius four-door. I live in West Virginia, but I'll call him and tell him where you are. OK?"

"Yeah, my name is Ricky and we'll wait here."

"What are you wearing so I can tell him what to look for?"

"I'm wearing a red tee shirt and white shorts. Joey is wearing a blue tee shirt and blue jeans We will be here Please tell him to hurry "

"OK, end this call and I will call you back when I reach him. "

I continued to call Gene on his work phone but there was no answer.

The two guys with Gene's phone did not know Gene's ringtone. A call came through on his phone and the ring tone was a man's voice singing "Jesus, Jesus, do you know Jesus; Jesus, Jesus, do you know Jesus."

Joey noticed on the screen the caller ID read "Ruth Ann Cell"

As soon as Joey said "Yeah", Ruth Ann said, "I've seen all the text from you and Richard. Are you OK?"

Joey told her what had happened concerning finding the phone on the side of the highway.

Ruth Ann said, "Oh my goodness."

Joey continued "I have been talking to RichMac who was talking to the person who owns the phone. The call with RichMac did not end."

"My name is Ruth Ann. Both RichMac (his name is Richard) and Gene are my brothers.

"Well, Richard is trying to get hold of Gene on his work phone in order to direct him to where we. "

Suddenly Ruth Ann heard a screeching sound like tires skidding on the highway, a loud thud, and the call ended. She called Gene's phone again and it just rang and rang with no response. Before the call went to voice mail, Ruth Ann just ended the call.

Both Joey and Ricky went airborne when a white panel van suddenly hit them. The crash caused Gene's phone to go airborne slamming into the windshield of a 1972 red Ford Thunderbird traveling in the opposite direction on U.S. 19.

The two men landed on the berm in front of a CVS pharmacy. All traffic in the area suddenly stopped and calls from people in the area to 911 almost overwhelmed the emergency center. In moments, multiple sirens could be heard.

Gene was traveling south on U.S. 19 and got stuck in what seemed to be a parking lot. He called me from his work phone, and I said "Where have you been? Your phone has been found "

"Oh wow, "Gene responded.

My phone was interrupted by a call from Ruth Ann. I told Gene "Hold on, I'm bringing Ruth Ann in on the call. "

Ruth Ann related to Gene that she was talking to the guy who found his phone, but the call suddenly ended. Gene told Ruth Ann and Richard that he was in his car but there was a crash just south of where he was on the highway. RichMac said "I talked to the guy who has your phone too. He is at the intersection of Trouble Creek Road and US 19 and he's holding onto your phone."

Richard, Ruth Ann, and Gene continued to be amazed that the phone slid off Gene's car and was still working.

The paramedics who arrived at the scene of the accident went to where the two men were located. Local police were talking to the driver of the white panel van.

The driver of a Ford Thunderbird parked on the opposite side of US 19 did not know why a phone hit his windshield. The bottom corner of the phone hit the passenger side windshield and lodged in the glass. The driver of the Thunderbird waited until the light turned green and the pedestrian light appeared. He walked quickly to the driver's side of one of the two police cars to let someone know about the phone lodged in the windshield of his car.

The first paramedic to reach the two men saw the crimson stains not only on the shirt of one of the men but also the red stain in the grass near him. Both had landed near one another head-to-head. One man was on his back and the other was lying face down. The sudden thrust of the approximately 150-pound man caused his face to sink 6 to 8 inches into the grass He was motionless and appeared at first glance to be dead. The other man was still alive and the fingers on his left hand were twitching, and he was breathing with shallow breaths.

The paramedic who cared for the man on his back had an eerie experience a few days earlier when he participated in a training exercise with local police officers. The group of police officers and other emergency personnel watched training films, but one video made an enormous impression on him. The film was from the body camera of a rural southern deputy who made a traffic stop on the highway. The small device pinned to the deputy's lapel picked up all the sound and video in front of him. As the deputy from the video was exiting his police cruiser, the driver of the stopped car exited his at the same time. The video depicted the driver holding a revolver in his right hand and the officer yelled "Put the gun down." The driver suddenly pointed the weapon at the deputy and fired one round. The deputy fired five rounds with his Smith & Wesson 40 caliber pistol. The driver dropped by his car and the deputy continued to walk toward the man he shot. The deputy was breathing hard and pressed the send button on the radio connected to the left lapel of his shirt to tell his communication center that he shot a suspect, and he needed help. The deputy was extremely emotional. He continued walking to the injured man and noticed he was still breathing. Blood was oozing from the man's right shoulder. The revolver he had been holding had been flung under his vehicle. When the officer knew he was safe and the man could offer no more harm to him, he shouted out in his southern draw "Do you know Jesus, do you know Jesus? You may be meeting Him soon." The video indeed.

The paramedic was overcome with a need to say the same thing to the victim he was tending to, and he said in a resounding manner "Jesus, Jesus, do you know Jesus? Jesus, Jesus, do you know Jesus?" The victim softly uttered, "Answer his phone." Again, the paramedic said, "Do you know Jesus, do you know Jesus" and again the victim answered quietly "Answer the phone."

The police officer who was investigating the accident approached the driver of the white panel van to find out what happened to cause the van to hit the two men. The man was very emotional and had been crying over and over.

He almost shouted out "I was listening to an evangelist on the radio and he was preaching about the Holy Spirit working on the heart of people and convicting them of their sins and to pray to the Lord and ask Jesus to come into their hearts. I just got so emotional, and I wanted to trust in Jesus. I threw my hands in the air and the next thing I knew; I had run over two men. Oh my God, I'm so sorry. Is there anything I can do to help them? How may I tell them I'm sorry? "

The officer said "Not right now. They both have been transported to the hospital."

"But are they going to be OK?" the man asked.

"This just happened," the officer said, "and I don't know the condition of either of the men. We will find out because I must take you to the station to get a written statement from you. We will have to tow your van to the police department to continue with the investigation."

"I'll do anything." the man driving the white panel van replied.

The man from the Thunderbird got to the police car and stopped beside the driver's side door of the police car. The officer recognized him and lowered the window.

"Can I help you?" the officer asked.

A tall middle-aged man wearing blue jeans and a Tampa Bay Buccaneers tee shirt said, "At about the same time those two men were hit by the white van, a cell phone fell from the sky and lodged in the windshield of my Thunderbird over there across the street."

He pointed across the highway and continued, "The bright red one, but the strangest thing is that when this happened, a voice from God startled me."

"What do you mean?", the officer asked.

The voice said "Jesus, Jesus do you know Jesus? The voice repeated this several times and I was shocked. Then all the traffic slowed down and I pulled over to the side of the road when I saw all the flashing emergency lights. I thought the crash of the phone into my windshield may be connected to these two men ".

At the hospital in the emergency room, Joey was attended to by the ER-resident physician who had just arrived at work. Joey was cleaned by two nurses and his shirt was cut to allow the medical professionals to decide if he had wounds on his chest or abdomen. The right side of his head had been shaved by the paramedics and a compression bandage was placed on the wound on his head just above his right ear.

"Sir, can you hear me?" The doctor asked.

Joey shook his head up and down indicating the affirmative response.

"What is your name?" the doctor asked.

"Joey Lockhart," he responded.

"Do you know what happened to you?"

"No, all I know is that I was standing along the road and I woke up in the grass."

"Where do you feel pain," the doctor asked.

"I have throbbing pain in my upper left leg." Joey responded.

The doctor pressed on Joey's body and watched and listened to responses from wherever his hands were pressing on the man's flesh. Joey made the most grimacing response when the doctor pressed on his upper left leg.

Let's give him 50 of Demerol and when he is stabilized x-ray to get a look at his upper left leg." the doctor ordered.

Ricky was dead on arrival at the hospital. His body was transported to the basement at the morgue where the medical personnel looked for any information the man may have had in his pocket to determine if he was an organ donor.

Joey arrived at the nuclear medicine department and a technician addressed him.

"Hello, I'm Heather and I'll get you in here as soon as possible."

"Thank you, ma'am," Joey responded.

Heather asked, "What have you learned most from the entire experience you've encountered?"

Joey said, "I know I need Jesus in my life."

TEACHERS

R ichMac had been a fan of the English rock band Pink Floyd for many years. Although he liked all the music of Pink Floyd, he was especially fond of the eleventh studio album "The Wall" released in November 1979 by a British recording company. RichMac played the two CDs often while driving in his car and he was thrilled by the lyrics of the fourth and fifth songs on the first CD about teachers and education. The lyrics of the two songs portray mercenary teachers who hurt children and instructions for dealing with the mean teachers. Specifically, the fifth song alluded to a wall and an illusion that each brick in the wall represents teachers.

Teachers do not harm children, but it made RichMac think about the education system in West Virginia which appeared to be in disarray. He, like some other community members, had opinions on what needed to be done to repair the dilemma, but not what to do specifically. Legislators and school officials had opposing impressions on settling the controversy and clearing up the docent's controversy. Some educators expressed a desire for traditional education methods while more liberal views gave the nod for charter schools which receive government funding but operate independently of the established state school system in which it is located.

Older and mature voters in the community did not know why teachers no longer evoked corporal punishment in classrooms. RichMac was of this persuasion and could remember when the paddle with holes in the board had whacked the behind of many students whose behavior was discreditable

There were others who seemed to be persuaded by the notion of autodidactic learning.

"I grew up to become a productive citizen", RichMac thought, "and I was a member of that generation of students who got corporal punishment".

RichMac remembered when his social studies teacher in junior high school gave a female student the option of paddling for an infraction committed or sticking her nose in a ring drawn on the chalkboard for 30 minutes. She chose to place her nose in the ring on the board.

Were poor conditions in some schools the fault of teachers, school board members, legislators, the governor, the court system, or parents? Why were the state schools in last place compared to other states in national statistics for learning?

RichMac thought about this issue, and he concluded that there must be some way to bring the matter to the people to begin discussing how to resolve the problem of education. He guessed he might have an idea about some way to get people to become aware of the matter so all interested residents could communicate with school board members to pass along ideas for a better education system. Additionally, RichMac believed that the school system needed input from as many teachers as possible who were on the front line of the education system.

He recognized the need for much support for solving this problem as well as capital to pay for his brainstorming idea. He searched the internet for a list of community members who were philanthropists, particularly those who favored scholarships, apprenticeships, and pedagogy. One person who stood out above all the others was Earl Rogers a self-made millionaire who had worked his way up the schooling ladder to attain a Bachelor of Science degree, master's degree, and ultimately a doctorate degree.

RichMac wrote to Mr. Rogers to explain that he (RichMac) believed that the entire populous should get interested in schools and provide ideas for the best education system for the state. Additionally, he related that there should be an alliance with the teachers for input compared to what changes they believe should be made to address the obstacles. He included in his correspondence with Mr. Rogers the description of his idea of a popular rock song by a faddish 1970s rock band (Pink Floyd) that might get the attention of the citizens as well as the media. The two-page letter was mailed in certified mail, return receipt was asked. RichMac included his address, phone number, and Facebook and Twitter accounts. He provided Mr. Rogers with potential dates, times, and various locations to meet to begin discussing what RichMac believed were excellent ideas.

He created an organizational plan with the steps for accomplishing the goal and a budget for acquiring all items necessary for achieving the strategy. He learned that West Virginia has approximately 20,000 part-time- and full-time teachers. Additionally, he wrote to the West Virginia State School Board Superintendent requesting the best day of the week for all teachers to be away from their responsibilities for one day. He sought the sum of money needed to pay all the teachers their salary for one day while away from their jobs and the amount per diem to cover all expenses for travel, meals, and lodging. RichMac also called the Charleston Coliseum and Convention Center to discuss with management the best day of the week to house a large event for several thousand participants.

To the budget, he listed 20,000 boxes with an inside width of 4 inches, an inside length of 10 inches an inside depth of 3 inches, and 20,000 standard bricks. He planned to use the bricks to illustrate how many bricks to make a wall made by teachers. He included colorful wrapping paper and ribbons for the list._

RichMac received a letter from Mr. Rogers which included his phone number and a request for RichMac to call his personal secretary to schedule a date and time for the two to meet at Mr. Rogers's office. He checked his calendar and called the secretary explaining that he had plenty of time to meet with Mr. Rogers and requested several dates he would be available. She provided RichMac three potential dates and the first one on April 22 was selected.

At 9:00 AM on Tuesday, April 22 RichMac appeared at Mr. Rogers's office for the planned meeting. A nameplate on the desk of an attractive young lady read "Judy Alexander". She was speaking to someone on the telephone and raised her right index finger as she looked at RichMac to give him notice that she would be with him in a moment. After a few minutes, she placed the phone on the receiver.

"Yes sir, may I help you?" Ms. Alexander asked.

"Yes Ma'am", RichMac responded, "My name is Mr. RichMac and I have a meeting with Mr. Rogers."

"Please have a seat Mr. RichMac and I will let Mr. Rogers know you are here."

"Thank you ma'am", RichMac answered.

In approximately five minutes a tall man wearing a blue pin stripped suit entered the foyer area of the office behind Ms. Alexander.

"You must be Mr. RichMac", the tall gentleman stated extending his right hand for a handshake. "I am Earl Rogers. Please follow me into my office."

RichMac followed Mr. Rogers into an office that seemed to be as large as four rooms at his house. He was directed to a very comfortable Hamburg Armchair.

"Mr. RichMac, I read your letter and I appreciate your willingness to get people interested in the education system for our state so the government and the current school administrators may make the best decisions for educating our children.

"Thank you, sir."

"I am old enough to remember the music of Pink Floyd and I especially enjoyed their album titled "The Wall." I just do not see the relationship between this rock group and getting citizens stirred up about education. Can you help me understand that?"

"First of all Mr. Rogers, thank you very much for giving me your time to discuss this matter".

"The plan in a nutshell is to have all the teachers meet in the coliseum of the Charleston Civic Center. As each one enters the coliseum a small box containing a brick wrapped in beautiful wrapping paper with an attractive bow will be provided to each teacher with strict orders to wait till the order is given later on that day for each to open his or her "gift" when directed to do so. The meeting will begin with the State Superintendent explaining to the teachers that the school board needs to have as many residents as possible and voters to become energized to think about what the school system needs to become a great center of education for the state's school children. An open-ended survey will be provided to all teachers for their opinions on what they believe to be the best ideas for a productive school system. Later, the same day music from PINK FLOYD's "THE WALL" relating to teachers and the bricks will hopefully portray the song's message. This expectantly will be covered by the media so the public will hopefully understand the need to speak to local school boards. I believe that this nontraditional method of getting ideas from teachers and the citizens of our state will assist those who implement the education plan for our state.

"Mr. RichMac, I like your idea and I am willing to support you, but have you spoken to any state school officials about what they think about this?"

"Yes, I sent a letter to Mr. Noddingham, the Superintendent of the West Virginia school system, and met with him about the matter. He liked the idea too but his concern was the cost of taking the teachers away from the classroom even for one day."

"I believe we can solve that problem", Mr. Rogers explained.

"Do you mean the cost of salary of the teachers for one day?" RichMac asked.

"Yes", he responded.

"Now, about the music", Mr. Rogers said, "I know David Gilmour of the group well. He was one of the original members of Pink Floyd when they published and performed "The Wall." I will reach him and ask if the group can perform here in Charleston. I am sure that will generate much interest from the public. All the nearly 20,000 teachers will be able to attend at no cost. I recommend that the meeting with the teachers before the concert be in a separate venue for them to complete the surveys. The boxes holding the bricks can be provided to them at the meeting with the superintendent and be used as their entry fee for the concert."

"That is great Mr. Rogers. I will decide with the scheduling office at the Colosseum and Convention Center and put the representative from Pink Floyd in touch with the civic center to take care of the details of the event. I'll wait to hear from you about the band's performance.

"Here is my business card with my cell phone and e-mail address so we can keep in touch with each other." Mr. Rogers related. "I have all your contact information and will certainly let you know after I talk to David."

"Thank you very much", RichMac responded.

RichMac called Mr. Noddingham's office to set a time to meet with him again to explain what had materialized since he talked to him last. He decided to go to the Colosseum and convention center and speak to the scheduling department about a space for the meeting with the teachers as well as the large concert event.

Two weeks passed and Mr. Rogers called RichMac to inform him that he had spoken to David Gilmour and he was very interested in making this happen. According to Mr. Rogers, Pink Floyd had to work out the details for such an event and get back in touch with him. The tentative date for the event would be September 25.

"If you will e-mail me the name and e-mail address of the person from the Colosseum and Convention Center to provide to David, the two entities will be able to work out the details on the scheduled day." Mr. Rogers said.

Finally, on June 22 the details for the September 25 event came to pass. The state school board had communicated with all 55 county boards of education and all teachers had been informed of mandatory attendance at the meeting The person RichMac had been communicating with at the Superintendent's office and representatives of the West Virginia Education Association related that there was generally positive feedback from teachers, however, there were a few who expressed disdain for such an event

On September 20th RichMac, Mr. Rogers, Mr. Noddingham, and the President of the West Virginia Education Association met to finalize the details of the event. All were especially grateful for what had been done to promote the event. RichMac related to the group that he was extraordinarily gracious for the willingness of Mr. Rogers to cover the costs of the meeting and concert. A suggestion by Mr. Rogers to give to Habitat for Humanity all the bricks used was heralded by all those who attended.

Volunteers from elementary schools throughout the state stepped up to place a brick into a box and decorate the boxes with glamorous wrapping paper and attractive ribbons and bows. The boxed bricks were collected and stored in a rented storage unit near the civic center for use on September 25.

At 9:00 AM on September 25, 18,560 teachers from throughout West Virginia were seated in the coliseum. The speech by Mr. Noddingham lasted for approximately 15 minutes and the open-ended surveys were passed out to each of those in attendance. During the time it took to pass out the surveys, the concept of the bricks in the boxes was explained to them, including how during the Pink Floyd concert they would be asked at a certain time to remove the bricks from the boxes. Stacked boxes near the exit to the right door of the coliseum were pointed out to the group. Take one each Mr. Noddingham explained. These will be your "tickets" to get into the concert tonight. They were all asked to take a break after completing the survey and go to one of the five meeting rooms on the first floor of the civic center by noon where lunch was going to be served.

RichMac and Mr. Noddingham met with members of the press to apprise them of the purpose of the event to influence as many citizens as possible to meet with their individual county school boards. This meeting would be useful to provide to the school board their opinions of what they believe the board should be doing for the education of children in the various counties.

At the luncheon, teachers were reminded that the doors to the coliseum would be opened at 5:30 PM and the concert would begin at 7:00 PM. They were reminded to arrive with the box provided.

RichMac met with Mr. Rogers who was backstage with members of the singing group. He was introduced to David Gilmour and other members of the group who would be performing in the evening.

When the coliseum doors opened, teachers were filing in to get a good seat. Each one who entered had a decorated box in his or her arms. By 6:45 PM it appeared that all the teachers had arrived. A few very young people were probably given a box by a teacher who did not care about listening to the Pink Floyd concert.

Pink Floyd was introduced by Mr. Rogers at 7:00 PM sharp and the music began. The first song in the album "In the Flesh" was played followed by "The Thin Ice." Those songs were followed by "Another Brick in the Wall Part 1", "Mother", "Goodbye Blue Sky", "Empty Spaces", "Young Lust", "One of My Turns", "Don't Leave Me Now", Another Brick in the Wall part 3", Goodbye Cruel World", "Hey You" and "Is There Anybody Out There."

At that time an intermission began and continued for about 20 minutes. There was some droll behavior when members of the group got up from their seats and carried the decorated box with them to the concession stand or the restroom. All the food items during the concert were complimentary. Before the music resumed, Mr. Noddingham asked the teachers to open their boxes and hold the brick and, in a few moments, nearly all the teachers were sitting in their seats with a brick in their hands.

The music began again with "Nobody Home" and "Vera." These were followed by "Comfortably Numb", "The Show Must Go On", "In the Flesh", "Run Like Hell", "Waiting for the Worms", "Stop", "The Trial" and "Outside the Wall"

The last two songs set the stage for the bricks. The first song led up to the bricks. It was "The Happiest Days of Our Lives followed by "Another Brick in the Wall, part 2." When the show was over many television cameras and correspondents began wrapping up their filming of the concert and the teachers. They exited the coliseum to wait for teachers for interviews. Mr. Noddingham came to the microphone again reminding all participants to leave their boxes in their seats and to place the bricks along the wall near the exit. By midnight the coliseum was empty of participants and only the cleanup crew picked up the boxes and paper in the seats. The bricks were left on the floor till the following day.

Over the next month, more than 5,000 citizens visited their various boards of education state-wide and attended board meetings for many months later The results of the surveys were analyzed and the data was used in drafting new legislation for the state education program

Two years later West Virginia was rated number 3 compared to other states in national statistics for learning. The West Virginia Department of Education was visited by 35 other states to glean what information they could learn from what West Virginia had learned. The greatest treasure was that students in West Virginia ultimately excelled in what they learned.

Detective Call Out 1

Police detectives are on call after hours when crimes occur. When I had first began working as a police detective my partner and I were called at home early in the morning to report to the address of a death. Several detectives were present when my partner and I arrived. The crime scene needed to be photographed by the forensic team including a drawing of the scene for the investigation. The victim was a young white female that I had known previously when investigating drug cases. She had provided information to the Drug Unit officers about people who were dealing drugs near where she lived. She was married and her husband was on the scene to report what had happened. It turned out that the uniform police officers who had arrived initially at the crime scene allowed the husband to go to the bathroom to wash his hands. This action prevented gunshot residue from being detected on the hands of the husband. The senior detectives discussed the need to have this matter as part of training for police officers to remember if they took part in a similar case.

The weapon was lying on the bed next to the victim. They had been arguing about their married life and she vowed to kill herself with the firearm. It was a Smith and Wesson 357 magnum revolver with a 6-inch barrel. He related that she was promising to commit suicide because she did not think her life was worth living. He said that near the end of their discussion and before the gun was fired, he was begging her to put the gun down.

"That's the last time I charged at her and I got my right hand on the trigger guard of the weapon, but she still had it in her right hand pointing it under her chin. We struggled for about 2 to 3 minutes and suddenly it discharged in her lower neck area. We both had hold of the gun when it went off".

After all the measurements had been drawn and the photographs taken, the detective sergeant said "We need to roll her over to see what is under the body."

She was lying on her back and her knees were bent and hanging over the side of the bed. Her head was turned to the right and her eyes were open. There was very little blood around the wound at the bottom of her neck. The detective sergeant got his hands under her right shoulder while another detective held onto her right knee. Together, they pushed and turned her to the left with her face down on the bed. As her body was being turned a sound like an extremely loud moan blasted out from the turning body for all of us to hear and it continued till she was fully rolled over. The thundering moaning sound at once frightened me. I was thinking "Is she still alive?" At that same moment, the detective sergeant said in an admonishing tone scolding tone, "Oh, shut up! A smile formed on the detective sergeant's face as he was looking at me.

He said, "When the foreign object entered her body and severed the top of her aorta the blood began spilling into her body cavity with each heartbeat till nearly all her ten pints of blood in the body settled in the body cavity making the sound we heard. According to the Detective Sergeant, it was that massive amount of blood pressing on all the internal organs and making a groaning-like sound.

After the medical examiner's office picked up the body, we took the husband to the police station to get a statement from him. He explained that when he grabbed the weapon with his right hand, he had all his fingers around the barrel trying to point it at the floor. She was trying, according to him, to raise the end of the barrel to under her chin.

After a few days, two other detectives and I met with the chief medical examiner at his office to conclude the manner of death and cause of death. He said three possible things could have happened to cause the death. He added that his decision could be detrimental to the husband or to the life insurance company that managed a policy for the victim. It was either suicide, homicide, or accidental death. He paged through the file and said I do not know how to conclude with the case resolution.

"Therefore, the four of us," he said "are going to take a piece of paper and write one word on the paper. Write suicide, homicide, or accidental. Whatever the majority agrees upon will be my determination for the cause of death".

I wrote accidental death, and all the others wrote the same.

Detective Call Out 2

At approximately 3:00 AM I received a call from the police department to come to work on an armed robbery at the Fifth Quarter Steak House Restaurant to investigate an armed robbery. The patrol officers on the scene at the restaurant introduced me and the other detectives to the manager of the business as well as the cleanup man who was the victim of the robbery. The manager explained that after the restaurant closed for business a man came into the restaurant wearing a ski mask and carrying a large revolver.

The assailant had stuffed something in his mouth to prevent him from talking. The manager said the robber kept his teeth clenched and only mumbled something about getting money from the safe. The looter followed the manager and the cleanup man to the safe. When they arrived at the safe the masked person pointed at the gun, he was carrying it, showing that the manager should open the safe. When the safe was opened, the cash inside was removed and given to the robber. Then the manager and the cleanup man were directed to go to the restaurant freezer and remain there for an hour before coming out.

I interviewed the cleanup man and learned that the robber was wearing two ski masks to prevent being found, but both masks, according to the cleanup man, were stretched tight across the nose exposing a small amount of dark complected skin. We started narrowing down our suspects to African Americans.

The manager stated that the robber was also wearing gloves, so we had no opportunity to seek fingerprint evidence. The manager was provided with our names and asked to call us if he happened to uncover any new information. We gathered the reports written by the uniform patrol officers and went to the detective division to continue the investigation.

Later that same day the manager called the detective division to speak to me. He told me that one of his employees found in a waste can a wet crumpled-up paper towel that appeared to have been in someone's mouth. He asked if we wanted it and I told him we did and instructed him to prevent other employees from touching the evidence.

The paper towel was picked up and taken to the medical examiner's (ME) office with the intent of having the chief medical examiner make a cast of the impressed paper towel. He was a highly skilled professional and had even taken part in the dental examination of Lee Harvey Oswald when the body was exhumed in 1981. Oswald, who was the chief defendant in the assignation of President John F. Kennedy and a Dallas, Texas police officer in November of 1963, was shot and killed by Jack Ruby.

The Chief ME was able to make a cast of the paper towel, and a sample of the paper towel was extracted to determine the blood type of the person who had the paper towel in his or her mouth. At that time DNA could not be used for criminal examination and investigation and only a range of blood types could be estimated for a group of people.

The ME said that if a plastic cast of a suspect's teeth was available, he could compare the cast developed from the paper towel with the cast from a suspect.

There had been much discussion among the restaurant employees about the robbery and the manager had instructed all employees to report any information they might have about the incident. An employee who worked in the kitchen area related to the manager that a former employee he worked with brought to work one evening a .357 magnum revolver and showed it to his coworkers. The manager called the detective division to report this information. The former employee, according to the manager, was fired for being constantly late and not performing satisfactorily. He was an African American male. The manager provided the former employee's name to the police department. His name and date of birth matched prison records for a convicted felon serving time for burglary seven years earlier. The man was on parole but had no recent criminal events.

The employee who provided the information to the manager was brought to the detective division and a detailed statement describing the firearm he saw the former employee with was obtained for the case file.

The results from the police crime lab about the blood type obtained from the wet paper towel showed the individual's blood type might be A positive. There was no way to narrow it down to exactly one person's blood type. A review of the records from the West Virginia State Penitentiary for the suspect revealed he had A positive blood type. With this information, we had a meeting with the prosecuting attorney about the case and we asked if he thought a judge would sign a search warrant to allow us to force the suspect to submit to having a dentist to obtain a plastic cast from his teeth. The attorney in the prosecutor's office had a staff member type a complaint and warrant for the judge to examine. The sitting judge on duty was approached and he agreed that it was plausible to believe the suspect's teeth might match the cast developed by the medical examiner.

My colleagues and I in the detective division discussed where we might find a dentist who would be willing to make a dental impression. My family dentist had been a proponent of the police and an enmity for crimes and criminals. I told this to the other detectives, and they agreed my dentist should be notified initially.

I called my dentist and asked when he would be available to discuss a police matter. He told me to come see him in about an hour. In his office, he listened intently to the facts of the case and the need for the teeth impression. He stated he would be willing to make an impression, so we worked on the logistics to find the best time to find the suspect and take him to the dentist for the impression.

On the appointed date the suspect was found, and the search warrant was shown and explained to him. He said he had nothing to hide and agreed completely to go with us to the dentist's office. He sat the suspect in the dental chair and explained every step to him.

The dentist said, "I'm going to place a thick liquid material called alginate into an impression tray that is shaped like a U in order to properly fit into your mouth. The liquid material will harden in a few hours when it comes out of your mouth, and it will be used to compare to another substance. This has caused the gag reflex for some people, but we're going to go very slow, and I don't think you will have any constraints when I get finished."

The procedure went smoothly, and the hardened impression was submitted to the ME's office. It took him about 10 days to complete the comparison of the two impressions and when he was finished, he emphatically said the two impressions matched identically.

A grand jury report was prepared for the prosecutor's office and the following month I appeared before the grand jury to testify to the facts of the case. No jurors asked any questions of me, but when they had finished, the defendant was indicted for armed robbery. He was found and arrested for the crime detailed in the formal accusation and his bail was set at 50,000 dollars. He was able to get out of jail to await the trial date scheduled for seven months later.

The case was put in the filing cabinet waiting for the trial date. There were discussions with the defendant's attorney about a plea of guilty and avoiding a trial, but the defendant wanted to go to trial and not plead guilty. The closer the date of the trial became reality; I called the dentist to let him know he would be getting a subpoena for appearance as a witness in the trial. He told me he understood and after the trial began, he was told what day to come to the courthouse for his testimony. The room where witnesses were held up had a private restroom, and a small kitchenette, well-ventilated and well-lighted.

The dentist arrived at the courthouse at approximately 0800 for his testimony. He expected to testify early in the morning and get released about an hour after arriving. He did not get to testify till approximately 1545, and he was only on the witness stand for less than 60 seconds. He had been a fan of the Perry Mason television show, and he imagined he would testify for 15 to 20 minutes. He also thought he would only be at the courthouse for an hour. When the jury finished their proceedings, the defendant was convicted and sentenced on the same day to 50 years in prison. I called the dentist to thank him for his service in the trial. He appeared to be agitated about his time spent at the court and reiterated that I was to never call him again for technical or professional assistance. He said he canceled many patients that he could have seen when he was just sitting all day in the witness room. I explained to him that I had no control over when witnesses were selected for testimony and often the prosecutor must juggle witness presentation before the jury when the defendant's attorney offers testimony that will extend the trial. He reiterated that he wanted no calls ever again to call him as an expert witness in a criminal or civil case.

THE DIARY OF A SAILOR

My Navy experience began in early 1967 when I signed my enlistment document committing to four years of military service. I had to report in May of 1967, so I had a few months to take care of my civilian affairs before beginning my military service.

I left on a Greyhound bus from my home in Charleston, West Virginia to the Recruit Training Center in Great Lakes, Illinois near Chicago. As the bus left the bus station, my family was gathered along with my girlfriend waiting for the bus to depart. They were crying and I did not know why. I was going on a bus trip to what I thought was a leisurely vacation and they were teary-eyed because I just might return to the same bus station in a body bag as a casualty of the war in Vietnam. The military draft did not take me into the Army like many of my friends, however since my father was a sailor just 25 years before this in WW II, I knew what I wanted to do. Besides, my uncle had enlisted in the Navy during the Korean War.

The trip to Chicago took all day and the bus stopped many times in small towns to pick up passengers in Ohio, Indiana, and Illinois. We arrived at the Greyhound station very early in the morning of the next day and I had to run off the bus and through the massive station to find the men's room. In a corner of the men's room were the longest row of urinals I had ever seen in my life, and I caught a glimpse of what I thought was homosexual solicitation in the bathroom. As I was relieving myself a man walked up to a urinal at once to the left of where I was urinating and began looking down and to the right and smiling. I thought to myself 'He is looking at me for God's sake'. The son of the devil was looking at either the rate of speed my bladder was forcing urine into the porcelain fixture, or he was trying to look at my penis. I had not experienced that kind of behavior in West Virginia, or I had just not seen it. I gave him a look of disgust and the weirdo got the message that I was not interested in getting to know him.

I returned to the main concourse and found a large white sign mounted about ten feet high and mounted to a huge colonnade outside a large glass door. The words "U.S. Navy Recruits Here" were written in large black letters. Under the letters was an arrow pointing to the space on the concrete floor next to the large pillar. I sat my bag down and three minutes later another young man sat a bag down near mine. He said, 'You going to Great Lakes too?' I smiled and nodded, and he told me he was from North Carolina. He removed a pack of Winston cigarettes from his shirt pocket and offered me one. I thanked him and declined. He lit the cigarette and began smoking. Not more than two minutes later a gray bus with

"Great Lakes Naval Training Center" written along the side of the vehicle appeared along the curb and the door opened. The guy from North Carolina got on the bus first carrying his bag and I followed him. There were about twenty young men on the bus already and I sat in an empty seat immediately behind the boy from North Carolina. We arrived at the main gate of the naval base and a neatly dressed Marine Corps sentry waved the bus to proceed. When the bus stopped just inside the main gate a sophisticated U.S. Navy Petty Officer entered the front door of the bus and stared at the young man in front of me who was smoking a cigarette. His stare lasted for more than 15 seconds and suddenly with all the authority of the United States Government he screamed "Put out that cigarette, you're in the Navy now!" That statement made a huge impression on my interpretation of freedom for the next two and one-half months.

A holding facility was home for approximately two weeks while others and I waited to go to an official Recruit Command Company. Every other person existing on the base wore a Navy or Marine Corps uniform, except for us. We were arrayed in blue jeans, sweatpants, dress pants, or anything else we had brought from home. It just did not seem right, but that's the way it was!

A friend of mine from years gone by told me a story once about the great white whale. He said, 'This whale is the largest mammal on earth, and it has only a throat about this big'. He curled the fingers on his hand next to the fingers of his left hand and touched the heel of his hands together forming a lumen about two inches in diameter. He said, 'And you know what, that's the way it is'. And it was!

"We all learned very quickly to hurry up and wait. Everyone was in a hurry for us to get everywhere, but many times after arriving at our destination, we had to wait for an hour or two. In the meantime, sinks, toilets, floors, equipment, bedding, and many other things needed to be cleaned, folded, waxed, shined, or tended to in some manner. While we did these tasks, the naval personnel tried very hard to break our will or so it seemed. Some of them were very mean. For instance, some of the personnel watching over us took great care to be violent and, in many cases, to inflict pain by assaulting us. A very good way to command attention was with the push-ups. The petty officers commanded us to get into the push-up exercise position and they took the order very seriously. At times when a recruit thought the petty officers were not watching, they would sink down and rest their knees on the floor. But Petty Officer Ratinoll somehow could see the violation, and he would scream out "You little baby", so everyone knew one of the recruits was caught. But it did not end there. Ratinoll would slowly walk over to the captured soul who got caught and with the force of a 49-yard field goal kick, he planted the toe of his right shoe into the rib cage of the victim. The sound was loud too! I do not know if Ratinoll practiced this kick, but it had a sound like the smashing of bones along with a sudden blown tire. You could hear the bones crunch. The next sound was the groaning by the victim recruit because of the pain. I learned quickly to never touch the floor with my knees when ordered to do push-ups. And this little game Ratinoll played with our minds was a conquering mechanism. It made me understand who the boss was really quickly. Two fellow recruits, Michael Leonelli and Daniel Webster did not fare as well. The hearsay was that they were going to be medically discharged. Ratinoll had broken them down mentally. They were misfits. They could not take it. I guess it would be a similar environment as a prisoner of war, and maybe that is why the ranking officers condoned this behavior.

Two weeks to the day after arriving at Great Lakes I was assigned to Recruit Training Command, Drill Company 5933. The recruit training began June 12, 1967, and ended August 11, 1967. There were 47 of us in the new company and our commander, Machinery Repairman First Class J. L. McClafin made us think he was the Chief of Naval Operations straight from Washington DC. The words he uttered that stood out most in my mind were "dive" and "dung face". The words were quite apropos to the situation. He was charged with getting a whole flock of recruits into ship shape before committing them to the campaign in Southeast Asia. He, like Ratinoll, knew how to get a young man's mind in the right direction. He told us to dive when he wanted us to lie prone on the floor in the push-up position with our arms extended. We got used to that word. I believe you can torture a man in this manner. The pain that develops in the triceps and bicep muscles is the formation of lactic acid, which is the product of glycolysis, or the conversion of glucose to lactate and pyruvate. This provides energy anaerobically in skeletal muscles. Who cares what it is? I just know that while doing push-ups the pain is so severe a man will do anything to avoid that agony. First Class J.

L. McClafin gave us all a name while in this hellhole. It was a "dung face". Every recruit in the company was referred to as a dung face. I used to ponder how one human being could demoralize and deject another human by calling him a dung face.

"Dive you dung face mongrels", he yelled when he was fuming about anything.

We took a dive for anything that made McClafin uncomfortable. It finally sunk in my thick skull one day that McClafin told us to dive to prepare us for war. I realized that an officer in an emergency on board the ship did not want to take time to tell me why I should take a document to the captain or why he needed the speed of the ship to change from all ahead full to stop in a matter of seconds. When that realization began making sense, the time in boot camp passed so fast. It all began to be meaningful to me and more importantly, the job that fate made me a more suitable person.

The entire dilemma of becoming a sailor and going to Viet Nam developed my life for the future. I cherish the experiences during those four years in the Navy. They were there for a purpose, and because of that, or because of that, I was always in the right place at the right time.

Immediately after boot camp, I became a Seaman, an E-3. I was transferred to a basic electric and electronics (BE&E) training school with the intent of going to Radarman School. The BE&E training, a prerequisite for the radar school, lasted for 16 weeks and the instructional material provided each week built upon the knowledge gained from the previous week. In addition, there was no room for mistakes, so anyone who failed a weekly test was abruptly transferred from the training to a navy ship as a boatswain's mate. The fear of rejection and peer pressure was always paramount, and the job of boatswain's mate was analogous to Satin's first mate in Hades according to the instructors in the BE&E training.

Each of the weekly exams consisted of thirty multiple-choice questions with a, b, c, or d as the correct answer. A cardboard answer key was placed on the exam answer sheet to grade the test. Holes in the answer key were aligned with the correct answer to figure out if the response to the question had been blackened with a number 2 lead pencil. The instructor grading the exams used a red ink pen to make a mark in the holes where a correct answer was not blackened. The red was as noticeable as the crimson letter Hester Prynne wore on her dress. Each of us in the training knew that missing more than 10 of the 30 questions was automatic expulsion and we had to stand in front of the podium while the instructor graded the exam. My heart raced with consternation while the petty officer graded each of my exams. Every week I counted the red marks as they were scratched on my answer sheet through the answer key. After the fourth week of exams, I watched as the red marks were slashed, one after the other. I counted 2, 3, 4, 5, and 6 till my heart sank. The racing heart turned to total numbness and my stomach did a flip-flop. At 8, I dropped my head and waited for the humiliation, but he stopped at 9 and I loathed the pain I knew that was forthcoming from the following week's exam. When a Seaman did not make a weekly grade, the petty officer scoring the exam disgraced the poor soul feverishly with tormenting words.

'Smith sure screwed up. No wonder. Any bastard from Arkansas can't pass this training'. The petty officer told Smith he was an idiot and directed him to the office to find out when he would be shipped out.

We don't want screw-ups like you here', the petty officer declared.

It was so emotionally humiliating to Randy Smith that he began crying. The tears were barely noticeable at first, but slowly they ran down his large nose and dripped on the floor.

'Well, well, besides an idiot, Smith is a crying little boy too', the petty officer exclaimed.

I saw the horror appear on Randy Smith's face. I really thought he was going to push his hand through the smile on the petty officer's face, but instead, he turned and walked away.

The petty officer showed about as much sensitivity to Smith's dilemma as a mob of MADD mothers to a drunk driver found in his car on a school playground. I wanted to hate that man. He was mentally ruthless.

Somehow, I passed all 16 weeks and was transferred to Radar School for 24 weeks. The intensity of the training was greater, but there were mentors available if one found he was slipping behind. I suppose the Navy figured that if they had this much time invested in us it was worth getting sailors through the course. Many of the instructors were former radarmen from ships that had served in Vietnam. We heard stories about tracking as many as 30 jets at one time on the radar screen when massive bombing raids were underway.

'How in the name of Heaven could I possibly do that when I was struggling to track just one plane in the training?' I used to think to myself.

'Practice, practice, practice! This is the key. 'Art Linkletter once said if you practice one thing every day for one year, you will become an expert at it', Second Class Petty Officer Jeff Bodner often said.

The 24 weeks progressed along very quickly, and by the time I graduated, I could easily track 25 aircraft at one time. Jeff Bodner told the families and friends of our graduating class that I was an outstanding student and would make any ship's Captain proud to have me as a new radarman.

My first ship assignment was the U.S.S. Horne (DLG-30) homeported in San Diego. California. It was one of the newest floating war machines developed by the United States. The U.S.S. Horne departed for the Western Pacific on May 29, 1968, from San Diego, California, and was headed by Captain Stansfield Turner. Captain Turner was relieved of his duty on July 26, 1968, by the new captain, Captain Archy L. Lupia. Captain Turner was ultimately appointed Director of the Central Intelligence Agency by President Jimmy Carter in February 1977.

The return date was scheduled for the first week of December 1968. I was specifically assigned to the operations (OI) Division where all the radarmen worked.

The ship stopped at many locations on Earth in sailing to the western Pacific. The first place the ship stopped was in Hawaii.

The first place the ship stopped was in Hawaii at Pearl Harbor. While on the ship, I had the added duty of working for the commander of Destroyer Squadron 21. In times of war, a commander of a squadron is assigned the rank of commodore. The commodore has the awarded rank of captain but is recognized as Commodore just below the rank of Rear Admiral. I was assigned to be his driver. When the ship arrived at various ports in the world, I had to drive him from the ship to his desired locations. The next stop and the trip to Vietnam was the Philippines. The port we docked at was in Subic Bay. Other locations we stopped at included Yokosuka, Japan, and Hong Kong.

When the ship arrived in the Gulf of Tonkin off the coast of Vietnam the ship relieved the vessel that had been there for several months to do search and rescue acting as a watchtower guiding the navy aircraft from their carriers to their targets and back and helping to rescue pilots in distress.

My Job, like other radarmen was to track the bombing aircraft that were assigned to the aircraft carriers in the Gulf of Tonkin. The duty was usually 12 hours on and 12 hours off. This duty lasted till the middle of November 1968 and the ship traveled east across the Pacific Ocean stopping in Hawaii and finally in San Diego.

During the trip home in the fall of 1968, the ship crossed the equator, and we participated in the Ceremony of the Imperivm Neptvni Regis or crossing the equator. The men who had crossed previously were referred to as Shellbacks and those who had not Pollywogs. The line-crossing ceremony commemorates a person's first crossing of the equator.

When the ship arrived in San Diego, I took leave and went back to West Virginia and proposed to my girlfriend. We set a date of January 19, 1969, to be married. I stayed on the ship all of 1968 and after the marriage we traveled by automobile from West Virginia to California where I had secured an apartment in National City, a suburb of San Diego. During our stay there together, she became pregnant with our first daughter. During the last trimester of the pregnancy, she moved back to West Virginia and a few days before the baby was born, I took leave and was home when my daughter was born.

When I returned to San Diego, I moved out of the apartment and back to the ship.

I learned of a transfer procedure where a sailor can petition for a transfer if he or she finds someone of the same rating on a similar ship and a different port. When I learned that a sailor on a ship in Charleston South Carolina who was from San Francisco California wanted to transfer with someone on a ship on the West Coast of the U.S., we began communicating with one another and completed the necessary forms for the transfer. Nearly 3 months later, the transfer was made. The sailor was a third-class radarman on the USS Wainwright DLG-28. We had to pay for the trip, and I transferred to the USS Wainwright DLG-28 homeported in Charleston, South Carolina. I was happy because it was closer to home.

Since the ship's job was like any job in America with a time to begin work and a time for the workday to end, many Seamen and Petty Officers had apartments in downtown Charleston or one of the surrounding municipalities. I, on the other hand, chose to stay in my U.S. Navy bunk, which was free of charge. One Seaman in particular who had an apartment in North Charleston fascinated me. Romulus Stephens was from California, and he seemed to be what the news media, magazines, and other sources described as a hippie. The outside of his apartment was just like that of any row of apartments on the street where he lived. The inside was a different story. The aroma of incense was so pungent upon entering his abode that it mimicked the thickest fog I had ever seen in West Virginia. The music was almost exclusively The Doors, and the speakers were so loud the reverberating sound taunted my chest cavity making me feel each breath of air that filled my lungs. Someone had stolen a tombstone from a cemetery and it was sitting up in the living room with brown army blankets folded in a manner to portray the actual gravesite. On the ceiling, large black and white squares were painted like floor tiles and on the wall, a trumpet had been uncoiled to extend from one corner to the other. Each window was fancied with cheap K-Mart draperies. Over each set of drapes was a piece of thick black industrial-strength plastic to keep any light from entering the windows. Every lamp in the living room had a black light screwed into the socket under the shade, and on the mantle was a blaring strobe light. Several joints that had been rolled for what looked like a long time were in a plastic baggie on the mantle with another baggie holding what appeared to be two or three ounces of marihuana.

Romulus seemed to love his life away from the ship and, deep down, hate his time while on board the iron haze gray war machine.

He was a little shorter than me, about 5 feet 9 inches tall, and he had a little flab in his abdominal area, which made it appear that he had always been overweight. His black hair and black mustache were as much a part of him as was his whole being, but the thing that stood out the most was his demeanor. He hated the government, and particularly the police or any law enforcement agency anywhere. If a person was associated in any manner with the police, Romulus made an example of the poor soul by riding him hard and putting him up wet. I kept my mouth shut about my father's job, even though it was a small police agency in a very rural state. I knew Romulus would not trust me if he knew where my father worked. He told me how the police spray mace on people. When I asked him about how this mace thing worked, I erred by asking him how the police threw mace at people.

He got mad and corrected my terminology, 'The police spray mace, they don't throw it, you goofy mongrel!'

He called anyone who was a friend of the police a Narc'.

'According to Romulus, that was a slang term for someone who revealed evidence to a Narcotics agent of the use, sale, or possession of illegal drugs. I had never heard the term before. I knew as much about being a narc as I did about the theory of relativity. Once when we were walking to his apartment, he referred to the young man with long hair in the back seat of the marked food police car as a narc.

'Never trust a narc', he said, 'They will rat you out in a second'

Romulus and I worked together for two years, and my father's job was never revealed.

The operational experience of being on a ship, as well as the training I received in boot camp, BE&E, and radar school, put things into perspective for me, almost as easily as did A.J. (my father's nickname). It was not the fear of screwing up that got my attention; it was always doing the right thing that genuinely made an impression on me. I became a Navy addict. The Navy was the only real thing that meant anything to me. If the U.S. Navy declared that urinating in your gas tank was the correct thing to do, you know where I would be peeing when my bladder was full. The sense of allegiance to God and country, but mostly 'doing the right thing' set the precedence for the kind navy sailor I turned out to be.

As I mentioned previously, our ship was underway across the Pacific Ocean to ultimately Viet Nam When the ship returned to San Diego, I learned of a procedure or program that enabled enlisted sailors on ships to transfer from one ship to another at no cost if the two sailors were going to swap positions of the same rank and did the same job I found a sailor who was a third-class petty officer like me who was stationed on a destroyer leader cruise ship at Charleston South Carolina The sailor worked as I did in the combat information center and was willing to move to the West Coast of the US since his home was in Los Angeles California The two of us communicated often by writing letters in the 1960s since there was no social media available at the time He was willing to pay the expenses to relocate to San Diego and I likewise was interested in moving to Charleston South Carolina since it was nearer to my home in West Virginia

The whole process took several months but I eventually moved to Charleston South Carolina and relocated to the operations and intelligence division sleeping quarters of the ship. It was the U.S.S. Wainwright DLG 28. When I talked to comrades in my division, I learned that the ship had just completed a cruise to Vietnam and was destined to go on a cruise across the Atlantic Ocean to the Mediterranean Sea. I was happy with that because I had just come from the western Pacific and took part six months in the war zone off the coast of Vietnam Nam in the Gulf of Tonkin. The orders were changed, and the U.S.S. Wainwright was to head again to the Gulf of Tonkin to Viet Nam.

Military personnel including members of the Marine Corps, Army, Air Force, and Coast Guard who took part in combat in the war zone were allowed combat pay as well as an exemption from United States Federal Income tax.

I remember that the U.S.S. Wainwright left on its 3rd and final deployment to Vietnam and final deployment to the western Pacific in conjunction with the

Vietnam conflict. Steaming via the Panama Canal and Pearl Harbor, the ship arrived in Yokosuka, Japan on 21 September 1970. For nearly two months, we conducted operations in the Sea of Japan with units of the Japanese Maritime Self Defense Force.

Periodically, while performing war tasks off the coast of Vietnam our warship sailed into Yokosuka and Sasebo, Japan for upkeep and liberty.

The ship left Japan on 14 November 1970 and headed via the Taiwan Strait for the Tonkin Gulf. On the 20th, we relieved the U.S.S. Jouett (DLG-29) the Positive Identification Radar Advisory Zone (PIRAZ) station and took up familiar duty as American air coordinator status in the northern part of the Gulf of Tonkin.

That assignment proved very brief, for on the following day, the U.S.S. Chicago (CG-11) relieved Wainwright and we moved on to new duties as the coordinator ship assigned to the North Search and Rescue (SAR) station. For almost a month, we alternated between north and south SAR stations, taking time briefly in mid-December to participate in Operation "Beacon Tower," a three-day exercise to test the readiness of American warships in the Tonkin Gulf to meet and deal with air and surface attacks. On 16 December, our ship left the combat zone, bound for Singapore, where our ship remained from 19 to 26 December. That was the first time in my life I spent Christmas in the Orient and the extremely warm weather.

From there we set a course for the Philippines and arrived in Subic Bay on the December 29th.

Our warship completed six days in port at Subic Bay and on 4 January 1970 we got underway for Hong Kong. She returned briefly to Subic Bay, however, for repairs to one of her radar antennae but finally reached Hong Kong on the 11th of January.

Following a four-day visit to Hong Kong, we left the British colony on the way to the Tonkin Gulf.

Wainwright served 16 days in the Gulf of Tonkin, dividing time between PIRAZ duties and assignments as the northern SAR ship.

After a final two-day stop at Subic Bay, Wainwright began the long voyage back to

Charleston, South Carolina which took her through the Indian Ocean, around the

Cape of Good Hope, and across the southern Atlantic to complete her first circumnavigation of the globe.

When the ship crossed the equator as it traveled south in the Indian Ocean off the east coast of Africa it was very warm. As the ship went south along the east coast of Africa it began to cool down. When we sailed along the southern coast of Africa around the Cape of Good Hope snow was in the air and the temperature had plummeted to below freezing. It was an extraordinary time to see the air temperature drop from the mid-80-degree range to freezing in just a few days.

Along the way, she made a series of calls to the Continents of Africa

and South America visiting various ports. One was Djibouti in French Somaliland. The country's name was changed to Djibouti in 1967.

The ship also landed in Massawa, Ethiopia, where she took part in the

celebration of the Ethiopian Navy Days, an annual celebration of Ethiopia's Navy. When Wainwright joined navy ships of other countries where midshipmen from the Ethiopian Naval Academy graduated, and we hosted Emperor Haile Selassie I on board our ship. Many years later when I shared my experience of being in the presence of Emperor Haile Selassie with a couple of Ethiopian professors, I worked with at Marshall University they looked shell-shocked. They asked me about him and wanted to know all the details. I equated the experience with speaking to someone from the United States who had met former President George Washington.

The Navy Days celebration included various sports events in which the sailors from various countries took part. At the time, I was young enough as well as strong and agile enough to participate in the 1 mile run competing with other naval personnel from members of various other countries.

An Ethiopian bus transported all the mile runners to the outskirts of the city one mile away. I sat on the bus with a sailor from the Soviet Union. We were unable to communicate with one another, but he recognized and pointed at the necklace I was wearing. It was a tiny photograph of my first daughter born in January 1970. We only smiled at one another and continued our destination outside of town. I completed the mile run; however, a young Ethiopian sailor crossed the finish line in almost record time surpassing everyone else.

Wainwright rounded out the African itinerary with ports of call at Diego Suarez, Madagascar, and at Lourenco Marques, Mozambique.

One experience I remember well when the ship stopped in Mozambique occurred when a sailor friend and I took a walk from the ship and beyond the city of Lourenco Marques, the capital city, where the ship was docked. It is interesting to note that this capital city's name was changed to Maputo in 1976.

We just wanted to explore the rural area of the city since we had only been exposed to a navy ship for several months. The city of Maputo was highly populated like other large cities of the world with many tall buildings. When we had walked several hundred yards away from the city, we noticed that the contour was like that of movies we had seen as children about Africa and Tarzan. We enjoyed the walk and the jungle atmosphere. Walking further and enjoying the sites, we noticed to our left a person walking at an angle toward us. We began talking about how we might communicate with the man or woman and how we might need to use abstract sign language to interact. As we neared one another we could tell that the individual was a very dark complected young black woman. When we were close enough to talk to one another the woman said in broken English "Hey sailor want to fuck"

We were devastated because we could hardly believe what we experienced while walking in such a beautiful bucolic area. She was quickly given a negative reply, and we continued our walk. We had both been exposed to that kind of behavior from women in bars and city streets all over the world in numerous ports of call. Both of us talked about this experience for a long time and related the experience to other colleagues on the ship. I am sure my companion told family members and friends when he left from his tour of service in the Navy.

As the ship sailed south in the Indian Ocean along the east coast of Africa, the ship crossed the dividing line on the earth that separates the northern hemisphere from the southern hemisphere called the equator. The line-crossing ceremony is an initiation right that commemorates a person's first crossing of the equator. The tradition may have originated many years ago to boost morale or to create a test for seasoned sailors to ensure their capability to manage long rough voyages. Equator crossing ceremonies typically featuring King Neptune (Roman god of the sea), are common in the Navy and are also sometimes conducted for passengers as entertainment on civilian ocean liners and cruise ships.

My most unforgettable experiences of crossing the equator occurred on both the navy ships I was assigned to. First was the U.S., Horne DLG-30 in the Pacific Ocean then while on board the U.S.S. Wainwright DLG-28 when it crossed the equator in the Indian Ocean while returning to the ship's home port at Charleston, South Carolina. Sailors who had never crossed the equator are referred to as pollywogs and those that complete the adventurous experience are called shellbacks. Many of my colleagues took part in the event. The inductees into the organization of the shellback had to CRAWL or walk on hands and knees from the bow of the ship to the stern a length of approximately 574 feet. We crawled along the ship's walkway with salt water from hoses keeping us wet on the ship. Those who had taken part in the event previously, the shellbacks, beat our hind ends with pieces of water hose. All along the ship's walkway, we were asked repeatedly, "What are you?" and the response was always "I am a pollywog." At the stern of the ship the oldest shell back on-board portrayed King Neptune and each of the pollywogs had to kiss his stomach that was greased with a thick black greasy substance. The last part of the event was being totally immersed in a cauldron of salt water and when the sailors raised their head from the water they were asked, "What are you?" The expected response was "I'm a shellback " But when a young man said "I am a pollywog" he was pushed back under the water and asked again till he finally understood that he was a shellback.

When the ship sailed around Africa and headed west in the Atlantic toward South America we first stopped in Rio de Janeiro, Brazil where we saw Ipanema Beach. That always reminded me of the song "The Girl from Ipanema" first recorded by Pery Ribeiro. The Brazilian lyricists wrote the song Antonio Carlos Jobim and Vinicius de Moraes in 1962. Being on Ipanema Beach was certainly a thrill for me in 1971. The statue of Christ, the Redeemer was also an immaculate sight to behold in Rio de Janeiro.

The other city in Brazil that was visited was Recife.

Before the ship arrived at the home port in Charleston, South Carolina on April 2, 1971, we made the last stop at St. Thomas in the Virgin Islands.

Shortly afterward, I made an appointment with the personnel department on board Wainwright and decided to complete my four-year military obligation.

and become discharged from the Navy. Because of President Richard Nixon's order to withdraw troops from Vietnam, I was able to leave the Navy for a few months. early before the end of my full four-year enlistment period.

SANDSPUR PLANTS

The backyard was covered in sandspur plants that were a nuisance for people and domestic animals. The spurs latch onto shoestrings, pant legs, and the pads of dogs and cats. Each spur is transported by various means for sprouting in many locations as a seedling. They are produced by GOD in HIS glorious world.

RichMac, a blood cancer and stem cell transplant patient were dealing with Graft versus Host Disease which manifested itself into Scleroderma and Dry eyes. He took his seven-day pill organizer out to the backyard to take his medicine. One of his medicines, one-half of a ten-milligram Prednisone tablet, fell from the pill organizer into the grass below. It landed between two sandspur plants and was easily seen because it was white between two green plants. He reached down to pick up the pellet and one of the sand spurs fastened to his right hand. He felt the pain from the spur in his finger and he saw the blood it produced. It did not seem as enterprising now about searching for the pill, but he wanted to fulfill his mission of picking it up. He was able to scrape the spur from his finger and using his foot, he mashed one of the two plants to the ground with his shoe so that it was not present when reaching down to pick up the pill. When the plant was smashed to the ground a white substance from the plant oozed out covering the ground including the half pill. He was not able to find where the tablet was found, but since the white substance from the plant covered the pill, he began pressing on the ground where he thought the pill was located to find it. When he thought he had found the half tablet he used his index finger and thumb to pick it up. He wiped the tablet covered with the white sticky substance on his pants till it was identified as the missing pill. He placed the pill in his mouth and swallowed it as well as all the other medicines that were in the seven-day pill organizer for Tuesday.

RichMac continued with his daily chores and left to go to Planet Fitness to do his daily workout. He felt good about how his legs and lungs were working while on the stationary bicycle. He believed something different was causing his body to react in a very positive manner.

"Could this be remnants of the white substance from the plant?" he thought.

Later in the afternoon, he did not feel that he needed to take a nap as he normally did. RichMac felt energized and much improved than he had at any other time before. He wanted to search on the internet to try to find information about the substance from the plant. In the meantime, he decided to mash more of the plants to get an added quantity of white material from the sandspur plants. He put on his gloves and went to the backyard where the greatest quantity of the plants existed. The plants were pulled from the ground and placed in a large plastic bowl he brought from the house. A Munchkin Go Mash Food Mashing Set was used to mash the plants in the bowl. The more he mashed the plants the more of the white substance appeared in the bottom of the bowl. When he had mashed five plants for about five minutes, the quantity of the white cream appeared to be about two tablespoons. The creamy substance was scraped into a small ceramic coffee cup. He retrieved his pill organizer and took out another one-half ten milligrams Prednisone pills from the container placed it in the coffee cup submerged it into the liquid and let the pill absorb the substance.

A few hours later when it was time to take his medicine, he took all his pills with water. The pill found in the creamy white substance was rescued and instead of wiping the liquid from the pill, he placed it in his mouth and swallowed it along with a cup of water. He decided to take a nap as he usually did after taking his medicine and relaxed on the reclining couch with his feet and legs elevated. He closed his eyes and laid his head back to get completely relaxed. As he was about to doze off to sleep, he noticed the time from the large clock on the wall in front of him as fifteen minutes till six in the evening. Later he felt a slight burning sensation in his groin area and both his feet were numb. He began to lift his right hand to feel what he thought was sweat on his forehead, but his hand and arm were inoperable. He could not lift his arms. The beads of what he thought were sweat began dripping onto his chest and each drop was crimson red. He suddenly dreaded the horror of what was happening, and he began to scream. No one else was home since he was living alone, and he did not know what he was going to do. He was sure that death would end his life and maybe no one would know what happened to him. He began to ask God for forgiveness for all his sins, but he knew he would end up in heaven since he was a born-again Christian who had given his life to Jesus Christ. The shirt he was wearing was engulfed in blood now and he began to become weak. He just knew that at any moment he would take his last breath.

Suddenly, the front doorbell rang, and he heard his brother's voice. It rang several times and was followed by the sound of the key entering the lock and opening the door.

"RichMac, are you OK," Gene asked.

"I need help. I'm in the TV room", RichMac responded.

Gene entered the TV room area and said, "My God, what happened to you?"

"I need help; I can't move my arms or legs."

Gene dialed 911 and told the operator who answered that his brother was bleeding and was incapacitated. Gene began looking for the source of the blood that was dripping from his brother's head. Gene got several towels and placed them on Rich Mac's head. He pressed hard to try to stop the bleeding but after a few minutes, the two towels became soaked in blood. Shortly afterward, the doorbell rang, and Gene raced to the door to let the paramedics in the house. They followed him to the TV room, and he told them RichMac could not move, but that blood was flowing from his head.

RichMac said, "I took a nap and woke up like this. I have cancer and I take a lot of medication, but this condition has never happened before."

"We need to have a list of your medication to give to the medical staff at the hospital." the lead paramedic said.

RichMac told Gene to go to the master bedroom and look on the shelf in the closet for a red cloth bag holding all his medication. He decided he did not want to tell them about the white creamy substance that came from the sandspur plants.

"What time did you take your last dose of medicine?" the nurse asked RichMac.

"It was just before six PM", he answered.

"The paramedics brought from your home a blue seven-day pill organizer with the medication arranged for morning and evening each day. It appears that the last pills taken were for today Tuesday in the evening. Is that correct?"

"Yes", RichMac acknowledged.

He hoped the paramedics and his brother found the white substance in the coffee cup at his house. He began to have feel in his right hand and just as quickly in his left hand. He raised his head and told the medical staff he was feeling better. The blood from his head stopped dripping and the bandage that had been placed on his head was removed and replaced with a new fresh bandage.

"The lab tests we did indicate you should not be alive." the physician tending to him told RichMac. "Your hemoglobin is below 5.0 and your hematocrit is the lowest I have ever seen. Your white blood count and platelets are extremely low too."

"I feel fine", RichMac said. "I was scared when all this happened, but I feel like I will be OK to go home now.

"We will repeat the lab tests to determine how your blood values are doing now", the physician said.

About 20 minutes later when the lab values were complete, the doctor said, "This is preposterous. Your lab values are all in the normal range. I have never seen anything like this before."

"Does that mean I can go home?" RichMac questioned.

"I do not see why not", the physician stated. "Let me see you walk."

RichMac sat on the edge of the bed in the Emergency Department and suddenly leaned forward. He dove off the bed, rolled on the floor and jumped up about three feet into the air. The medical staff watching him was amazed at this behavior and ran toward him, but he put his hands into the air in front of him signing that he was OK and did not need to be tended to.

His brother Gene helped him get his things together and they walked out to Gene's car together. During the drive home, Gene said, "You have had difficulty tying your shoes and bending over and especially standing up from a sitting position like on a couch.

The scleroderma has made you almost disabled. How in the world could you have done what you did at the hospital? It would have taken an experienced gymnast to do what you did when you jumped from the bed in the Emergency Room onto the floor."

"I just felt like doing it", RichMac said. He knew he could not tell his brother about the white substance from the plants, but he realized he would have some explaining to do at the Cancer Center at his next appointment when he told them he was no longer taking his medication. He called Dawn, his wife, to tell her he was cancer-free and no longer needed to be in the house he was renting from his brother to get the cancer treatment. He said he would be planning to drive back to West Virginia. RichMac poured the white substance from the coffee cup into the kitchen sink and no longer wanted anything to do with the substance.

At his next visit to the Cancer Center, one of the clerks registering him asked the standard questions including if he had been hospitalized since his last visit. He told the clerk about his experience, and she noted it for the medical staff to see. After his blood values were provided to the Physician's Assistant who saw him, she was amazed at how the blood values had changed to the normal range since he was in to see them previously. RichMac told her he had not taken any of his prescribed medication in two weeks. He said he felt wonderful and all the problems he had from the scleroderma were resolved. She had him place his arms above his head and put his palms together in front of his chest to see if he could raise his elbows in a horizontal position with the floor. She was amazed in concert with the lab values that he seemed to be free of any issues relative to myelodysplastic syndrome, Graft versus Host Disease, and Scleroderma.

He made his plans to leave the rental house and at the same time dug up several of the sandspur plants to take with him to West Virginia in case he needed them.

RichMac left the Tampa, Florida area and returned to West Virginia. Several months later he contracted the influenza virus and was confined to bed. His symptoms included body/muscle aches, chills, cough, chest pain, diarrhea, fever, and a stuffy runny nose. The first thing he thought of was the sandspur plants he had in his utility room. He kept the plants in a mild climate with plenty of water in case he needed to use them again. Dawn his wife had given him plenty of over-the-counter medicines to address the flu, but few things were working. While Dawn was away from the house, he made himself get out of bed and walk to the utility room. He secured a pair of work gloves that were on the hot water tank and walked to the pots holding the plants. He pulled three of them from the flowerpots and walked to the kitchen with them. He pulled a large plastic container from the cabinet and secured a device to mash the plants. The white substance began to appear in the bottom of the container, and he removed the glove, smeared a little of it on his finger, and placed it in his mouth. He returned to his bed and went to sleep. When Dawn returned to check on RichMac she found him unresponsive. She called 911 and the paramedics arrived to take RichMac to the hospital. He was pronounced dead on arrival.

He was interred in his family cemetery as his last will and testament had shown. The bottom half of the vault had been placed in the ground by the grave diggers in preparation for the deposit of the casket. The whole family and many of his friends attended the funeral and it was a very bleak setting. When all those who attended the funeral had left, the grave diggers placed the coffin into the grave and covered it with the top of the vault. The backhoe began filling in the sod to cover the grave site. Suddenly RichMac's left arm began moving and he opened his eyes in the darkness of the coffin.

THE CURING SOLUTION

RichMac was a cancer patient who was diagnosed with myelodysplastic syndrome in the spring of 2014. He migrated to the Moffitt Cancer Center in Tampa, Florida for treatment of the condition. In September 2014, he had a successful stem cell transplant, but he unfortunately drifted into the associated plight of graft versus host disease (GVHD). This action evolved into scleroderma and dry eyes. Cyclosporine Ophthalmic or Restasis solution had been a good remedy for RichMac's dry eyes. He began research concerning the mixture of other substances with Restasis. One example was a drop of water in the nose of a person who has frequent nosebleeds along with one drop of Restasis. According to the research, out of four hundred people who were included in the study ninety-one percent had successfully resolved the matter of nosebleeds. RichMac began to think this matter through thoroughly and wondered if other substances mixed with Restasis could resolve other ailments and infirmities.

Four years later, while taking multiple medications and having been diagnosed with GVHD, he had frequent bowel movements. Some of the bowel movements were classical causing some very embarrassing catastrophic events. One occurred while he was at an appointment at the cancer center. He had just had an EKG and was told to wait for the results of the procedure. While waiting, he had a sudden urge to defecate so he quickly walked to the restroom to take care of his business. As he was locking the door on the inside of the restroom a stool was gathered in his bowels and ended up in his underwear. That was followed by the second and third stools that traveled past his briefs and lodged in the leg of his jogger scrub pants with tight legs. Part of another stool found its way down into his left compression stocking. He sat on the toilet and removed his shoes to undress and remove the feces from his clothing. While doing so, part of one of the stools that had lodged in his scrub pants fell into his left shoe and onto the floor of the bathroom in front of the commode. It was a nightmare. The whole process took nearly forty-five minutes and while all this was happening there were five attempts by people trying to get into the toilet.

In early June of 2018, RichMac was with his brother and sister at a retail outlet looking for electronic products. He felt the urge to relieve himself while in the store, so he went to the men's room and entered the disabled stall area. While sitting on the toilet defecating, he noticed a large stain of thick feces in his underwear. He used a piece of toilet tissue to scrape the feces from inside his briefs. As he was scraping the feces, he noticed a bright crimson color mixed with the brown feces. This alarmed him and he looked at the stools in the toilet bowl for any blood but found none. He investigated the toilet after every bowel movement but never saw any bloody stools.

When he reported the blood in the stool to his healthcare team, a colonoscopy was discussed. One week later a colonoscopy and endoscopy were scheduled. The main preparation substance of four liters of NuLyely was bought at the pharmacy to deplete the colon of any hint of feces. RichMac began thinking of the studies using the Restasis and he wondered what effect the substance would have on the four liters of preparation substance. He had been drinking eight ounces of the preparation liquid at a time, so he placed a few drops of the Restasis solution into the liquid and drank the fluid.

When RichMac went to the toilet to expel the feces in his lower intestine he noticed for the first time a red liquid in the water of the toilet bowl. This discovery frightened him terribly. He knew this had to be from the Restasis since he had previously had bowel movements after drinking the preparation liquid and there was never any red substance in the toilet bowl water. He had a phone number for the Endoscopy Center, and he knew they encouraged any phone calls in preparation for the procedure. He called the number listed and asked to speak to someone about the procedure. He told a staff member about the blood, and he was informed that a physician would call him in a few minutes about the matter. When the physician called, he did not tell the doctor of the Restasis issue. He was told to continue to check the situation and report any added blood from the stools. RichMac decided to place several added drops of Restasis into the liquid to see what if anything might happen. At his next bowel movement, RichMac felt some larger-than-normal fecal matter pass through his rectum. When he finished, he glanced into the toilet bowl and saw bloody material that appeared to be intestinal tissue. He was in a panic over what he saw in the toilet. He decided he must retrieve some of the material from the toilet water and save it in case the medical team wanted to examine the material further. He took a perforated stainless-steel spoon from the kitchen and retrieved several pieces of bloody tissue from the toilet. He placed all that he had recouped into a gallon-sized zip lock bag.

He called the Endoscopy Center again and told the person who answered the phone the name of the doctor he talked to earlier about his issue. A moment later the same physician talked to him. The doctor told him to call 911 and go to the hospital emergency department for examination. RichMac told the physician about the material he captured from the toilet, and he was told to take that with him to the hospital. Before calling 911, he wanted to satisfy his need to go to the toilet once again. During this bowel movement, he felt a much larger mass pass through his rectum and splash so hard into the bowl that his buttocks were covered in water. He was distressed to look at the objects in the toilet but horrified when he detected what his mind could not comprehend. This time there was a similar amount of bloody tissue, but one much larger piece was covered in hair. It was the same color as the hair on his head. He again used the perforated spoon and placed the material into a separate gallon-sized zip-lock bag.

About twenty minutes later he was on his way to the hospital. The nurse who first communicated with him asked him to get on the scales to get his weight. He was hysterical when he saw that his weight was one hundred sixty-four pounds, a decrease of forty pounds in one week.

As he continued to hold onto the two zip lock bags, the nurse pointed at the bag holding the large piece of tissue with the hair and asked, "Is that a dead rat."

"No Ma'am" RichMac answered, "that came from my bowel movement."

"The doctor who told me to go to the hospital asked me to bring with me what was in the toilet after I had bowel movements."

RichMac told the nurse he had to go to the bathroom, and she pointed the way for him. He sat on the toilet and was afraid of what he might see in the bowl when he finished. He grunted and felt the movement. There was a great amount of passage through his rectum and as had happened previously he was afraid to look to see what had come from his body. It was another massive amount of tissue in the toilet, but he had no way of picking it out of the bowl. He just flushed the commode and returned to where the nurse was last located.

When he saw the physician at the emergency department, he told RichMac he needed to have a colonoscopy and RichMac told the doctor that he had a colonoscopy scheduled for the next morning. He told the doctor he felt well and was just prepping for the procedure for the next day.

On the day of the colonoscopy and endoscopy, a needle was inserted into the port in his chest and vital measurements were taken. The Anesthesiologist and Gastroenterologist discussed with RichMac all the necessary matters for the performance of the procedure.

RichMac told the gastroenterologist "I feel like I have nothing left in my lower colon from all the prepping that was done."

"Don't worry", the gastroenterologist told RichMac, "I hear that all the time."

Twenty minutes later the medical staff took RichMac back to the surgery center and anesthesia was provided to him. The gastroenterologist began with the scope of the lower gastrointestinal tract and then went ahead with the upper tract. RichMac was taken to the recovery room, awakened, and to the room for his family to visit with him and heard what the gastroenterologist needed to report of what he had found during the procedure.

He said, "I am amazed that you are still living and breathing. Nearly ninety percent of your lower intestine is gone. The terminal ileum, perianal and digital rectum, sigmoid colon, descending colon, traverse colon, ascending colon, cecum, and ileocecal valve are all gone. You should be dead. I have never had an experience like this previously in my career. Can you tell me what you think is the cause of this condition? All your vital signs are normal. I do not know why, but they are."

"Well doctor, do you know what Restasis is used for?" RichMac asked him.

"Yes, it is a medication for dry eyes, but what does that have to do with your GI tract?"

"You see, I put a few drops of the Restasis into the NuLytely solution as I was drinking it in preparation for the procedure."

"It just does not make sense. We will get the report from our laboratory on the items you brought in that were retrieved from your toilet after your bowel movements."

"OK, but can I go home now?"

"Sure. Once you are stable, your family members can drive you home; however, I want to see you in a few days to discuss this matter further. Someone from my staff will call you to decide on the date and time of the appointment."

RichMac knew he had to get this matter resolved and continue with his life, but the comment the doctor made to him about death upset him very much. When his sister took him home, he knew he had to try the Restasis again to see what else might happen to him. Since the prepping fluid was all used up, he decided to use sweet tea as an experiment to see what if anything might happen when he added Restasis to the tea. He poured a full mid-sized glass of sweetened tea and added four drops of Restasis to the liquid. RichMac stirred the solution well and drank the entire glass until it was gone. He felt a vibration in his mid-section as well as minor pain. He began to feel movement in his rectal area, but he had no desire to defecate. After about fifteen minutes all the minor pain was gone, and he felt fine.

RichMac reached the doctor's office for the appointment fifteen minutes before his appointment time. The receptionist greeted him and asked him to complete the information on the sheets attached to the clipboard. He completed the information and handed it back to her. RichMac was called to go back to the exam room and the doctor knocked on the door and entered.

"Hello RichMac", the doctor stated.

"Good afternoon, Doctor", RichMac replied.

"How have you been feeling? I discussed your condition with my coworkers and members of the American Society for Gastrointestinal Endoscopy (ASGE). The folks at ASGE would not believe me till I showed them your pictures from the scope I used for your procedure. I think our best bet is to schedule you for an MRI to affirm what my findings produced when you had the colonoscopy. The lab results from what you found in the toilet confirm they came from you based on your DNA.

"I have been feeling very well. But I do not understand why you found what you did when you did the procedure."

RichMac was examined by the doctor and was given the information on the date and time for the MRI. He got to his appointment early and was taken back to the Radiology and Imaging department of the hospital for an MRI. When the scan was complete, he was told he could leave and someone from the gastroenterologist's office would contact him.

He was called by the GI doc who told him all his organs were in place and had grown back. The physician added that he had discussed the results of the MRI with representatives of the ASGE and they wanted to interview him since no one in medical history had ever had such incredible results as he had experienced. RichMac told the physician that he did not want to take part in such discussions but just wanted to live his life without any agitation. He lived a long life and was never contacted by anyone further about this part of his life. He did use Restasis when he was diagnosed with other ailments, but the substance had no effect on his condition.

CRASH AND CONFESSION

R ichMac began his usual drive to the Moffitt Cancer Center in Tampa for treatment after he had been diagnosed with Myelodysplastic Syndrome approximately four years earlier. He was living in a rental home about one hour from the Cancer Center.

This drive was like all his earlier trips by automobile early in the morning with traffic increasing in volume as the day progressed. In his rearview mirror, he noticed a small red car driving erratically and attempting to pass any vehicle in one of the three lanes in front of him. This situation made him think of a car crash he saw a few weeks ago when an automobile side-swiped another car and both vehicles crashed into the median.

The small red car passed vehicles to the left and right and came within what seemed to be three feet of RichMac's car. The speed limit was fifty-five, but most drivers were speeding at between sixty to sixty-five miles per hour. The red car appeared to be driving at approximately seventy to eighty miles per hour. In a split second, the vehicle in front of the red car suddenly decelerated and the red car swerved to the left toward the median. As the red car continued toward the median it went on its side and began flipping several times until it came to rest upside down. The top of the car was crushed, and gasoline was seeping from the tank. Everyone slowly traveled on, but RichMac stopped in the median about fifty feet from the wrecked car. The smell of gasoline was very prominent. Another driver parked in front of RichMac and the two raced to the upside-down car.

Blood could be seen twenty feet away dripping from the driver's head. The driver's cranium was at the top of the driver's side window which was now upside down. Particles of glass were mixed in with the blood that was dripping. The driver apparently was not wearing a seat belt because he had been thrown with his feet against the passenger side door and his head leaning out the driver's side door shattered window. Several sirens could be heard from a distance showing that emergency services crews were on the way to the scene. The closer RichMac got to the wrecked vehicle the driver appeared alive because he was panting very quickly.

The other man who walked with RichMac to the scene said, "Do you think we should pull him out of the car"?

"No, I don't think so", RichMac responded. "He could have some neck trauma that could be worsened by pulling him out. And the jagged glass from the broken window may cause more lacerations to his face and head. We should use some clean cloth or paper towels to apply on his head where he is bleeding".

"I have some unopened paper towels in my car", the other man stated. "I will run back and get them".

"Great", RichMac answered.

The man began running toward his car and RichMac leaned down close to where the head of the man was found.

"Can you hear me?" he asked the injured man.

In a faint voice, the young man said, "Yes".

"Help is on the way," he told the man lying upside down in the car. "What is your first name son?"

"Lyle", he said.

"Lyle, do you know Jesus as your savior? Have you been saved?"

In a raspy voice, Lyle said "No".

"I am going to pray for you Lyle. Please just tell God that you want forgiveness of your sins, and you believe in Jesus as your savior".

"My grandma talks to me about that all the time".

"Ok, just tell God you believe Jesus is the risen Son of God and ask for forgiveness for all your sins.

In his scratchy voice, Lyle said, "Forgive me God of my sins and I believe that Jesus is the risen son of God".

RichMac began praying, "Heavenly Father, please accept Lyle's soul into heaven if he does not survive this tragic accident and I pray that his name is written in the Lamb's Book of Life. Amen".

The other man arrived and began tearing the plastic from the roll of paper towels. Lyle was no longer breathing, and it appeared he was dead. The first paramedic unit arrived and parked in front of the wrecked car. The first EMT to arrive yelled at the other paramedic "We'll need the jaws of life".

A Deputy Sheriff arrived at the scene parking in the passing lane closest to the median with his emergency lights flashing and blocking traffic. The full-size LED light bar with flashing white lights directed the oncoming traffic to the right. He began walking away from his car with about a dozen orange traffic barricades to direct traffic away from the roadway behind his vehicle. RichMac ran to the deputy and asked him if there was anything he could aid the deputy with. The deputy thanked him for the offer but said he needed no help at the time. RichMac told him he understood and that he had seen the accident.

"Thank you", the deputy answered. "I'll be finished in a few minutes, and I will get your information shortly".

RichMac called the Cancer Center to let the healthcare personnel know that he was not going to make his appointment because of the accident. A fire engine arrived at the scene and the firefighters began assessing the crash scene for the location of the gasoline. The EMT told the others at the scene that she could get no pulse or respiration from the victim. The police officer walked back to his cruiser, and he motioned for RichMac to come to the car. He entered the back seat of the police car and began providing information to the deputy. The erratic driving by the victim was explained in detail and the deputy entered the information into his MX 50 Notebook Tablet mounted on the dash located in the police vehicle. RichMac's personal information was provided to the officer so he could be contacted later if necessary. He walked back to his car and the deputy motioned for the man who retrieved the paper towels in his car to come to the police vehicle.

RichMac entered his car and eased off the median to travel the opposite way to go back home since he had to reschedule his appointment at the Cancer Center. He watched the news when he arrived home and learned that the accident he witnessed was a fatality. No name was provided but he knew the man's name was Lyle.

The next day RichMac began following the obituaries in the newspaper to see if he could find out more about the accident and subsequent death. On the following day, Mister Lyle Leeper was listed in the local Obituaries as the victim of the single vehicle crash two days prior on the highway where RichMac had stopped. The obituary said that Lyle was twenty-two years of age when he was killed in the crash. He graduated from New Port Richey High School and attended the University of South Florida where he graduated with a degree in business administration. Lyle was working for the State of Florida as a business assistant in Land-O-Lakes, Florida. The obituary said that he was survived by two siblings, a mother and father as well as both grandparents. It appeared that he was not married and had no children. A notation in the obituary showed that "In lieu of flowers, please make donations to the Pasco County Animal Shelter". The funeral service was scheduled for three days later at a funeral home in New Port Richey. RichMac noted the location of the funeral and particularly the time for the visitation before the funeral service. He wanted to find the grandmother Lyle referred to just before he died.

The visitation before the funeral was scheduled from six PM to eight PM. RichMac arrived at the funeral home at approximately five forty-five and looked for a parking spot near the building. There were very few cars in the parking lot, so he just sat in his car to get his thoughts together before going inside. At six PM, he exited his car and walked to the entrance of the funeral home. He noticed a signature book sitting on a counter just inside the large room where the coffin was found at the forward part of the room. There were about five signatures in the book. The family appeared to all be at the front of the room near the coffin. RichMac tried to imagine who the parents were as well as the grandparents. All of them were weeping and all were holding white tissues to wipe the tears from their eyes. He decided to stand near the rear of the room and just see what was happening. A middle-aged, well-dressed man wearing a blue pinstriped suit was talking with one of the women in the family who may have been a grandmother. The middle-aged man seemed to be consoling the woman, however, it seemed that every two to three minutes she broke down and cried. Some of the cries were loud and others in the room were looking at her. Each time she cried the middle-aged man placed his right hand on her shoulder; however, when she was bawling and blubbering the man hugged her to express sympathy.

RichMac decided to get a little closer to the family to pick up what he could hear. Since his goal was to locate the grandmother Lyle had referred to, he watched the two elder women. The greeting line was extremely long, and it had wound out the door and originated in the parking lot.

The woman who was talking to the middle-aged man said to him, "Pastor, I had many conversations with Lyle about his soul and his need to accept Jesus as his personal Savior".

"You planted the seed, and it was necessary for him to take action", the pastor related to the woman.

"I just know he did not go any further with this and I know his outcome. He is in hell" she yelled as she sobbed in great distress.

"There's no way for us to determine that Minny", the Pastor explained.

RichMac knew that it was time to approach Minny and let her know what had happened at once after the accident. He stepped in front of a lady who was in the visitation line as she turned to speak to the gentleman behind her. There were about four people in front of RichMac approaching the family. Minny was however sitting down next to the pastor continuing to sob and wail. RichMac approached the row of chairs where Minny and the pastor were sitting. After a few minutes, he caught the attention of the pastor.

"Hello, my name is RichMac, sir. I could not help overhearing the conversation you had with this lady, and I believe you are a pastor, is that right?"

"Yes, I am John Phillips, and I pastor a church in New Port Richey".

"Well, I need to talk to both of you because I was at the accident scene, and I talked to Lyle before he died".

The pastor's eyes opened widely, and they looked like a deer in headlights. He at once got the attention of Minny.

"Minny, I want you to hear this man. He talked to Lyle before he died at the accident scene".

"What happened?" Minny asked, almost screaming.

"I asked Lyle first if he could hear me and in a faint voice, he said yes. I told him help was on the way and I asked him his first name and he told me 'Lyle'. I said to him, Lyle, do you know Jesus as your savior? Have you been saved? In a raspy voice, he said no. I told him I was going to pray for him, and I asked him to ask God for forgiveness of his sins and to tell God that he believed that Jesus died for his sins and that Jesus was his savior. Then he said 'My grandma talks to me about that all the time.

"Oh my God. That's me", Minny said as she pressed her hand to her bosom.

"Well, he said he wanted Jesus to be his savior and to repent of his sins".

"This is the happiest day of my life", Minny said. "Oh, thank you sir for talking to my grandson.

"Well, his name is written in the Lamb's Book of Life now", RichMac added.

The visitation service continued, and the family members were ecstatic of the news RichMac had provided to them about Lyle's eternal life.

SALVATION AND LIFE

RichMac joined the men from his church to go to neighborhoods in the community to tell residents about their church and witness to them their relationships with Jesus Christ. The group RichMac was with went initially to a small ranch-style dwelling with most of the lights on to the left and right of the front door. The closer they got to the front door the smell of marihuana was quite recognizable. Joe, the leader looked at RichMac and Steve, the other man in the group showing he was going to knock on the door. When Joe knocked on the door the sounds from inside diminished and the music that had been very loud was suddenly muffled to a shallow murmur.

A white man wearing a ragged solid blue short-sleeved shirt had a tourniquet made from a rubber hose around his arm. He appeared to be about forty years old, and his brown hair was long and fell to the back of his neck. He looked exorbitantly thin, probably not more than one hundred forty pounds. The extended part of the hose was held tight by the man's teeth causing the tourniquet to be extremely tight. It was in place around his right bicep. A needle was dangling from a vein in his arm just below his bicep. When the man's eyes met Joe's eyes a sense of terror appeared on the man's face.

"Hello", Joe said. "We are from the church just around the corner and we are visiting our neighbors to let them know about the Lord's house. May we come in for a few minutes to tell you about our services?"

Reluctantly the man allowed Joe, RichMac, and Steve into the house. He quickly removed the needle from his arm and dropped the rubber hose from his arm. A woman yelled from a back room "Arnie, who's at the front door?"

The man who let the three representatives from the church in the house said, "It's three men from the church".

"As long as it's not the cops", the woman said.

The woman appeared in view of the men from the church. She was white and about thirty to forty years of age. She wore jeans and a yellow tank top. Her hair was a mess, and it appeared she had just awakened. She had a dazed look on her face and seemed to be intoxicated or high on marihuana. Arnie looked at her and asked her to come and join him on the couch. He did not offer a seat to the three men from the church. The woman sat on the couch with Arnie, and both looked at the three men from the church expecting some words about religion.

"This may not be the best time to visit with you", Joe said, "but we only want to let you know about our church and tell you about the love of God through Jesus Christ or the Lord. Did either of you go to church when you were growing up?"

The woman nodded her head affirmatively, but Arnie had no response.

"What kind of church did you attend and by the way what is your name?" Joe asked.

My name is Cindy, and it was a Baptist church. My mom insisted that my brothers and I go with her on Sundays. I was forced to go but didn't want to attend".

"Cindy, what is your relationship with Jesus Christ", Joe asked.

"I know who Jesus is. That's all we talked about in church. Jesus, Jesus, Jesus".

"Do you know where you will go when you die?" Joe asked her.

"OK, this is enough. This meeting is over, and you all can leave now", Arnie bellowed loudly.

"You just wait a minute Mr. Man", Cindy responded bitterly. "I do not mind talking to this man. I want to hear what he has to say".

"Ok, OK" Arnie reciprocated, "but just a few more minutes".

"Thank you, Arnie,", Joe stated. "We will be out of here momentarily. Now, getting back to my question to Cindy, where do you think you will end up when you die".

"I want to say Heaven", Cindy replied, "but I do not know for sure."

Joe looked at RichMac and asked if he would give her one.

RichMac removed a small Gideon New Testament from his pocket and gave it to her.

"If you open the testament to the back there are statements explaining how to become a Christian. You see first that God loves you and there are two bible verses that describe how we know that God loves us. Next is the fact that we all are sinners. Romans 23 twenty-three on page two hundred eighty-two explains that in detail. Even Billy Graham is a sinner. We all are, but God offered a countermeasure for the sin of mankind. The next statement 'God's Remedy for Sin' in the book tells us what God did to provide relief for mankind regarding a deliverance from sin. The verses listed in this section are proof that God did this for us. We must have faith and believe that the Bible is the Word of God. The next section tells us that 'All May be Saved Now'. And finally on the next page is how you can decide to receive Jesus Christ as your savior. What is your decision, Cindy? Do you want to become a born-again Christian"?

"Yes, I do", Cindy responded in a whimpering tone with tears in her eyes.

"Great, RichMac replied. I am going to read what is in the book about making a decision. Confessing to God that you are a sinner and believing that the Lord Jesus Christ died for your sins on the cross and was raised for your justification. Do you now receive and confess Jesus as your personal Savior?"

"Yes, I do", Cindy said.

"Let's pray", RichMac answered. "Dear Heavenly Father, thank you for this young woman and her decision to confess her sins and believe in your son the Lord Jesus Christ. May her name be written in the Lamb's Book of Life. Amen. Later, Cindy, you can write on this last page of the testament your name and today's date as when you accepted Christ as your Savior".

She continued to weep as she held the testament in her hands. She reached for a tissue in a box on the table next to the couch. During the whole time RichMac was talking to Cindy, Arnie was shaking his head with a stern look on his face. Suddenly in a moment of astonishment, Arnie pushed his right hand down between two cushions and brought into view a Smith and Wesson forty caliber pistol and pointed it at RichMac. In the next moment, he stood while holding the firearm and shaking it back and forth while pointing it at all three men simultaneously.

Joe had a frightened look on his face, and he told Arnie "Please let us go. We will leave immediately".

Arnie was mouthing something, but it was unintelligible. Saliva was dripping from Arnie's mouth onto the floor, and he continued to wave the pistol pointing it at all three men. Then in an undistinguished move and without any warning Arnie raised the muzzle of the pistol to his mouth and pulled the trigger causing him to fall to the floor with Steve's feet. The firearm fell on the couch a few inches from Cindy. She saw the pistol fall her way and she twisted her body to prevent it from falling on her. RichMac picked up the firearm and held it with his right hand pointing the barrel toward the floor.

"Arnie", she screamed.

RichMac removed his phone from his pocket and dialed nine one one.

"A man just shot himself in the mouth", he told the operator on the phone. "Cindy they are asking me the address. What is it?"

"Fifty-nineteen Grant Avenue", she replied.

RichMac gave the address to the operator and in the moments waiting for the authorities to arrive he felt a need to console Cindy since her husband or boyfriend had just committed suicide. The first emergency services representative to arrive was the police officer. Later, in a matter of seconds, the paramedics arrived. The officer had his firearm in his left hand, and he ordered RichMac to release the pistol he was holding in his hand.

"Place the gun on the floor" the officer demanded.

"Yes sir", RichMac answered. He placed the firearm on the floor in front of him.

"Now move away from the gun," the officer said.

RichMac and the other two men moved away from the pistol on the floor. Arnie was bleeding profusely and RichMac noticed that the back of his head was open and bleeding. The blood was mixed with Arnie's brown hair. RichMac looked at the ceiling in the room behind the couch and noticed a hole the bullet made when it exited Arnie's head. When the paramedics arrived, they placed Arnie on a stretcher and covered his entire body with a white sheet. RichMac, Joe, and Steve provided a detailed description of the events that evening and when two detectives arrived at the home, the three men provided written statements about what they witnessed. The officers were told that they were from the local church and were visiting people in the neighborhood and inviting them to the church. It was an evening RichMac would never forget.